THE BIBLE, THE JEWS, AND THE DEATH OF JESUS

A Collection of Catholic Documents

THE BIBLE, THE JEWS, AND THE DEATH OF JESUS

A Collection of Catholic Documents

Bishops' Committee for Ecumenical and Interreligious Affairs
United States Conference of Catholic Bishops

United States Conference of Catholic Bishops
Washington, D.C.

At its October 2003 meeting, the Bishops' Committee for Ecumenical and Interreligious Affairs discussed and approved the re-publication of the Catholic documents contained herein. The sources of these documents vary: one is from the Second Vatican Council, others are from Pope John Paul II and the Holy See, and yet others are from the United States Conference of Catholic Bishops (USCCB). This collection has been reviewed by Bishop Stephen Blaire, chairman of the committee, and approved for publication by the undersigned.

Msgr. William Fay
General Secretary, USCCB

Cover images: © Scott Speakes/Corbis.

Nostra Aetate excerpts from *Vatican Council II: The Conciliar and Post Conciliar Documents* edited by Austin Flannery, OP, copyright © 1975, Costello Publishing Company, Inc., Northport, N.Y. are used with permission of the publisher, all rights reserved. No part of these excerpts may be reproduced, stored in a retrieval system, or transmitted in any form or by any means—electronic, mechanical, photocopying, recording, or otherwise—without express written permission of Costello Publishing Company.

Excerpts from the *Catechism of the Catholic Church*, second edition, copyright © 2000, Libreria Editrice Vaticana–United States Conference of Catholic Bishops, Washington, D.C. Used with permission. All rights reserved.

Excerpts from the *Lectionary for Mass for Use in the Dioceses of the United States of America*, second typical edition © 2001, 1998, 1997, 1970, Confraternity of Christian Doctrine, Inc., Washington, D.C. Used with permission. All rights reserved. No portion of this text may be reproduced by any means without permission in writing from the copyright owner.

Excerpts from *The Historical Truth of the Gospels (Instructio de Historica Evangeliorum Veritate* (Latin-English text), translated by Benjamin N. Wambacq, O. Praem, *Catholic Biblical Quarterly*, Vol. 26, No. 3 (July 1964) © 1964, Catholic Biblical Association, Washington, D.C. Used with permission. All rights reserved.

Excerpts from *The Jewish People and Their Sacred Scriptures in the Christian Bible* © 2002, Libreria Editrice Vaticana, Vatican City. Used with permission. All rights reserved.

Excerpts from "Old Testament Essential to Know Jesus," *L'Osservatore Romano* (April 23, 1997) © 1997, *L'Osservatore Romano*, Vatican City. Used with permission. All rights reserved.

Second Printing, April 2004

ISBN 1-57455-618-5

Copyright © 2004, United States Conference of Catholic Bishops, Washington, D.C. All rights reserved. No part of this work may be reproduced or transmitted in any form or by any means, electronic or mechanical, including photocopying, recording, or by any information storage and retrieval system, without permission in writing from the copyright holder.

Contents

Introduction

On October 31, 1997, Pope John Paul II received a group of scholars attending a symposium on "The Roots of Anti-Judaism in the Christian Milieu," sponsored by the Holy See. He told them that

> erroneous and unjust interpretations of the New Testament regarding the Jewish people and their alleged culpability have circulated (in the Christian world) for too long, engendering feelings of hostility toward this people. They contributed to the lulling of consciences, so that when the wave of persecutions swept across Europe . . . the spiritual resistance of many was not what humanity rightfully expected from the disciples of Christ. Your examination of the past, in view of a purification of memory, is particularly appropriate for clearly showing that anti-Semitism has no justification and is absolutely reprehensible.

The members of the Bishops' Committee for Ecumenical and Interreligious Affairs of the United States Conference of Catholic Bishops echo the Holy Father in condemning anti-Semitism as sinful, and in deploring misinterpretations of the Sacred Scriptures for the promotion of anti-Semitic vilifications of Jews and Judaism. Therefore, the members of the committee decided to call attention to a number of significant Catholic teachings, and to do so in this publication, *The Bible, the Jews, and the Death of Jesus*. This publication brings together in one place excerpts from official documents of the Church pertaining to the interpretation of Scripture, anti-Semitism, and the understanding and presentation of the Passion and Death of Christ.

Two developments within the Church awakened and fostered a new understanding of the relationship between the Church and its roots in Judaism. The first was the biblical movement, which led the Church to a re-reading of the Gospels, and indeed all Scripture, through analysis of literary and historical forms, in order to identify a fuller theological understanding. The second development was that the Church in the Second Vatican Council formulated its commitment to re-examining its relationship with the Jewish people. Therefore, the readings included here first are from statements of the Council and from the Pontifical Biblical Commission. These define and develop how the Church reads her Scriptures in the light of Tradition. Continued efforts to better understand Judaism and to react to anti-Semitism have been made by the Magisterium as can be seen in the statements of the Holy Father, the Pontifical Commission for Religious Relations with the Jews, and the United States Conference of Catholic Bishops. As a part of this seeking for a better understanding of both the gospels and of Judaism, the Bishops' Committee for Ecumenical and Interreligious Affairs of the United States Conference of Catholic Bishops developed, in 1988, *Criteria for the Evaluation of Dramatizations of the Passion*.

Behind all these statements and gestures was the wish not only to end prejudices against Jews and Judaism, but also to to understand better the salvation in Christ by seeing the unique place of Jews and of the Jewish religion in the unfolding of salvation.

—Most Rev. Stephen E. Blaire, Bishop of Stockton
Chairman, Bishops' Committee for
Ecumenical and Interreligious Affairs,
United States Conference of Catholic Bishops

Statements of the
Second Vatican Council
and the
Pontifical Biblical Commission

Nostra Aetate: Declaration on the Relationship of the Church to Non-Christian Religions

Second Vatican Council
October 28, 1965

4. Sounding the depths of the mystery which is the Church, this sacred Council remembers the spiritual ties which link the people of the New Covenant to the stock of Abraham.

The Church of Christ acknowledges that in God's plan of salvation the beginnings of her faith and election are to be found in the patriarchs, Moses and the prophets. She professes that all Christ's faithful, who as men of faith are sons of Abraham (see Gal 3:7), are included in the same patriarch's call and that the salvation of the Church is mystically prefigured in the exodus of God's chosen people from the land of bondage. On this account the Church cannot forget that she received the revelation of the Old Testament by way of that people with whom God in his inexpressible mercy established the ancient covenant. Nor can she forget that she draws nourishment from that good olive tree onto which the wild olive branches of the Gentiles have been grafted (see Rom 11:17-24). The Church believes that Christ who is our peace has through his cross reconciled Jews and Gentiles and made them one in himself (see Eph 2:14, 16).

Likewise, the Church keeps ever before her mind the words of the apostle Paul about his kinsmen: "they are Israelites, and to them belong the sunship, the glory, the covenants, the giving of the law, the worship, and the promises; to them belong the patriarchs, and of their race according to the flesh, is the Christ" (Rom 9:4-5), the son of the virgin Mary. She is mindful, moreover, that the apostles, the pillars on which the Church stands, are of Jewish descent, as are many of those early disciples who proclaimed the Gospel of Christ to the world.

As holy Scripture testifies, Jerusalem did not recognize God's moment when it came (see Lk 19:42). Jews for the most part did not accept the Gospel; on the contrary, many opposed the spreading of it (see Rom 11:28).

Second Vatican Council, *Nostra Aetate*, no. 4 (October 28, 1965). In *Vatican Council II: The Conciliar and Post Conciliar Documents*, edited by Austin Flannery, OP. Northport, NY: Costello Publishing Company, 1975.

Even so, the apostle Paul maintains that the Jews remain very dear to God, for the sake of the patriarchs, since God does not take back the gifts he bestowed or the choice he made.[2] Together with the prophets and that same apostle, the Church awaits the day, known to God alone, when all peoples will call on God with one voice and "serve him shoulder to shoulder" (Soph 3:9; see Is 66:23; Ps 65:4; Rom 11:11-32).

Since Christians and Jews have such a common spiritual heritage, this sacred Council wishes to encourage and further mutual understanding and appreciation. This can be achieved, especially, by way of biblical and theological enquiry and through friendly discussions.

Even though Jewish authorities and those who followed their lead pressed for the death of Christ (see Jn 19:6), neither all Jews indiscriminately at that time, nor Jews today, can be charged with the crimes committed during his passion. It is true that the Church is the new people of God, yet the Jews should not be spoken of as rejected or accursed as if this followed from holy Scripture. Consequently, all must take care, lest in catechizing or in preaching the word of God, they teach anything which is not in accord with the truth of the Gospel message or the spirit of Christ.

Indeed, the Church reproves every form of persecution against whomsoever it may be directed. Remembering, then, her common heritage with the Jews and moved not by any political consideration, but solely by the religious motivation of Christian charity, she deplores all hatreds, persecutions, displays of antisemitism leveled at any time or from any source against the Jews.[b]

The Church always held and continues to hold that Christ out of infinite love freely underwent suffering and death because of the sins of all men, so that all might attain salvation. It is the duty of the church, therefore, in her preaching to proclaim the cross of Christ as the sign of God's universal love and the source of all grace.

Notes
2.   Cf. Rom. 11:28-29; cf. Dogm. Const. *Lumen Gentium* (AAS 57, 1965), 20.
b.   See D. 57.

Historical Truth of the Gospels
(*Instructio de Historica Evangeliorum Veritate*)

1964

2. In order to determine correctly the trustworthiness of what is transmitted in the Gospels, the interpreter must take careful note of the three stages of tradition by which the teaching and the life of Jesus have come down to us.

Christ our Lord attached to Himself certain chosen disciples[6] who had followed Him from the beginning,[7] who had seen His works and had heard His words, and thus were qualified to become witnesses of His life and teaching.[8] Our Lord, when expounding His teaching by word of mouth, observed the methods of reasoning and of exposition which were in common use at the time; in this way He accommodated Himself to the mentality of His hearers, and ensured that His teachings would be deeply impressed on their minds and would be easily retained in memory by His disciples. These latter grasped correctly the idea that the miracles and other events of the life of Jesus were things purposely performed or arranged by Him in such a way that men would thereby be led to believe in Christ and to accept by faith the doctrine of salvation.

The Apostles, bearing testimony to Jesus,[9] proclaimed first and foremost the death and resurrection of the Lord, faithfully recounting His life and words[10] and, as regards the manner of their preaching, taking into account the circumstances of their hearers.[11] After Jesus had risen from the dead, and when His divinity was clearly perceived,[12] the faith of the disciples, far from blotting out the remembrance of the events that had happened, rather consolidated it, since their faith was based on what Jesus had done and taught.[13] Nor was Jesus transformed into a "mythical" personage, and His teaching distorted, by reason of the worship which the disciples now paid Him, revering Him as Lord and Son of God. Yet it need not be denied that the Apostles, when handing on to their hearers the things which in actual fact the Lord had said and done, did so in the light of that fuller under-

Pontifical Biblical Commission, *The Historical Truth of the Gospels (Instructio de Historica Evangeliorum Veritate)* (Latin-English Text), no. 2. In *Catholic Biblical Quarterly* 26, No. 3 (July 1964).

standing which they enjoyed as a result of being schooled by the glorious things accomplished in Christ,[14] and of being illumined by the Spirit of Truth.[15] Thus it came about that, just as Jesus Himself after His resurrection had "interpreted to them"[16] both the words of the Old Testament and the words which He Himself had spoken,[17] so now they in their turn interpreted His words and deeds according to the needs of their hearers. "Devoting (themselves) to the ministry of the word"[18] they made use, as they preached, of such various forms of speech as were adapted to their own purposes and to the mentality of their hearers; for it was "to Greek and barbarian, to learned and simple,"[19] that they had a duty to discharge.[20] These varied ways of speaking which the heralds of Christ made use of in proclaiming Him must be distinguished one from the other and carefully appraised: catecheses, narratives, testimonies, hymns, doxologies, prayers and any other such literary forms as were customarily employed in Sacred Scripture and by people of that time.

The sacred authors, for the benefit of the churches, took this earliest body of instruction, which had been handed on orally at first and then in writing—for many soon set their hands to "drawing up a narrative"[21] of matters concerning the Lord Jesus—and set it down in the four Gospels. In doing this each of them followed a method suitable to the special purpose which he had in view. They selected certain things out of the many which had been handed on; some they synthesized, some they explained with an eye to the situation of the churches, painstakingly using every means of bringing home to their readers the solid truth of the things in which they had been instructed.[22] For, out of the material which they had received, the sacred authors selected especially those items which were adapted to the varied circumstances of the faithful as well as to the end which they themselves wished to attain; these they recounted in a manner consonant with those circumstances and with that end. And since the meaning of a statement depends, amongst other things, on the place which it has in a given sequence, the Evangelists, in handing on the words or the deeds of our Savior, explained them for the advantage of their readers by respectively setting them, one Evangelist in one context, another in another. For this reason the exegete must ask himself what the Evangelist intended by recounting a saying or a fact in a certain way, or by placing it in a certain context. For the truth of the narrative is not affected in the slightest by the fact that the Evangelists report the sayings or the doings of our Lord in a different order,[23] and that they use different words to express what He said, not keeping to the very letter, but nevertheless preserving the sense.[24] For, as St. Augustine says: "Where it is a question only of those matters whose order in the narrative may be indifferently this or that without in any way taking from the truth and authority of the Gospel, it is probable enough that each Evangelist believed he should narrate them in that same order in which God was pleased to suggest them to his recollection. The Holy Spirit distributes His gifts to each one according as He wills;[25] therefore, too, for the sake of those Books which were to be set so high at the very summit of authority, He undoubtedly guided and controlled the minds of the holy writers in their recollection of what they were to write; but as to why, in doing so, He should have permitted them, one to follow this order in his narrative, another to follow that—that is a question whose answer may possibly be found with God's help, if one seeks it out with reverent care."[26]

Unless the exegete, then, pays attention to all those factors which have a bearing on the origin and the composition of the Gospels, and makes due use of the acceptable findings of modern research, he will fail in his duty of ascertaining what the intentions of the sacred writers were, and what it is that they have actually said. The results of recent study have made it clear that the teachings and the life of Jesus were not simply recounted for the mere purpose of being kept in remembrance, but were "preached" in such a way as to furnish the Church with the foundation on which to build up faith and morals. It follows that the interpreter who subjects the testimony of the Evangelists to persevering scrutiny will be in a position to shed further light on the enduring theological value of the Gospels, and to throw into clearest relief the vital importance of the Church's interpretation.

—Benjamin N. Wambacq, O.Praem.
Consultor-Secretary
Pontifical Biblical Commission

Notes

6.   Cf. Mc. 3:14; Lc. 6:13.
7.   Cf. Lc. 1:2; Act. 1:21-22.
8.   Cf. Lc. 24:48; Jn. 15:27; Act. 1:8; 10:39; 13:31.

9. Cf. Lc. 24:44-48; Act. 2:32; 3:15; 5:30-32.

10. Cf. Act. 10:36-41.

11. Cf. Act. 13:16-41 with Act. 17:22-31.

12. Act. 2:36; Jn. 20:28.

13. Act 2:22; 10:37-39.

14. Jn. 2:22; 12:16; 11:51-52; cf. 14:26; 16:12-13; 7:39.

15. Cf. Jn. 14:26; 16:13.

16. Lc. 24:27.

17. Cf. Lc. 24:44-45; Act. 1:3.

18. Act. 6:4.

19. Rom. 1:14.

20. 1 Cor. 9:19-23.

21. Cf. Lc. 1:1

22. Cf. Lc. 1:4.

23. Cf. St. John Chrys., *In Mat. Hom.* I, 3; PG 57, 16-17.

24. Cf. St. August. *De consensu Evang.* 2, 12, 28; PL 34, 1102.

25. 1 Cor. 12:11.

26. *De consensu Evang.*, 2, 21, 51 s.; PL 34, 1102.

The Interpretation of the Bible in the Church
November 1993

[Intro, A] The historical-critical method, as its name suggests, is particularly attentive to the historical development of texts or traditions across the passage of time—that is, to all that is summed up in the word *diachronic*. But at the present time, in certain quarters, it finds itself in competition with methods which insist upon a *synchronic* understanding of texts—that is, one which has to do with their language, composition, narrative structure and capacity for persuasion.

[Intro, B] The Pontifical Biblical Commission desires to indicate the paths most appropriate for arriving at an interpretation of the Bible as faithful as possible to its character, both human and divine.

METHODS AND APPROACHES FOR INTERPRETATION

[I,A] The historical-critical method is the indispensable method for the scientific study of the meaning of ancient texts. Holy Scripture, inasmuch as it is the "word of God in human language," has been composed by human authors in all its various parts and in all the sources that lie behind them. Because of this, its proper understanding not only admits the use of this method but actually requires it.

[I,A,4] With respect to the inclusion in the method of a synchronic analysis of texts, we must recognize that we are dealing here with a legitimate operation, for it is the text in its final stage, rather than in its earlier editions, that is the expression of the word of God. But diachronic study remains indispensable for making known the historical dynamism which animates sacred Scripture and for shedding light upon its rich complexity.

[I,F] The basic problem with fundamentalist interpretation . . . is that, refusing to take into account the historical character of biblical revelation, it makes itself incapable of accepting the full truth of the incarnation itself. As regards relationships with God, fundamentalism seeks to escape any closeness of the divine and the human. It refuses to admit that the inspired

Pontifical Biblical Commission. *The Interpretation of the Bible in the Church.* Washington, DC: United States Conference of Catholic Bishops, 1996.

word of God has been expressed in human language and that this word has been expressed, under divine inspiration, by human authors possessed of limited capacities and resources. For this reason, it tends to treat the biblical text as if it had been dictated word for word by the Spirit. . . .

It often historicizes material which from the start never claimed to be historical. It considers historical everything that is [told] with verbs in the past tense, failing to take the necessary account of the possibility of symbolic or figurative meaning. . . .

Fundamentalism likewise tends to adopt very narrow points of view. It accepts the literal reality of an ancient, out-of-date cosmology simply because it is found expressed in the Bible; this blocks any dialogue with a broader way of seeing the relationship between culture and faith. Its relying upon a non-critical reading of certain texts of the Bible serves to reinforce political ideas and social attitudes that are marked by prejudices—racism, for example—quite contrary to the Christian gospel.

Finally, in its attachment to the principle "Scripture alone," fundamentalism separates the interpretation of the Bible from the tradition, which, guided by the Spirit, has authentically developed in union with Scripture in the heart of the community of faith. It fails to recognize that the New Testament took form within the Christian church and that it is the Holy Scripture of this church, the existence of which preceded the composition of the texts. Because of this, fundamentalism is often anti-church; . . . [i]t presents itself as a form of private interpretation which does not acknowledge that the church is founded on the Bible and draws its life and inspiration from Scripture.

The fundamentalist approach is dangerous, for it is attractive to people who look to the Bible for ready answers to the problems of life. It can deceive these people, offering them interpretations that are pious but illusory, instead of telling them that the Bible does not necessarily contain an immediate answer to each and every problem. Without saying as much in so many words, fundamentalism actually invites people to a kind of intellectual suicide. It injects into life a false certitude, for it unwittingly confuses the divine substance of the biblical message with what are in fact its human limitations.

HERMENEUTICAL QUESTIONS

[II,A,2] The Bible is the word of God for all succeeding ages. Hence, the absolute necessity of a hermeneutical theory that allows for the incorporation of the methods of literary and historical criticism within a broader model of interpretation. It is a question of overcoming the distance between the time of the authors and first addressees of the biblical texts, and our own contemporary age, and of doing so in a way that permits a correct actualization of the Scriptural message so that the Christian life of faith may find nourishment. All exegesis of texts is thus summoned to make itself fully complete through a "hermeneutics" understood in this modern sense. . . .

To avoid, then, purely subjective readings, an interpretation valid for contemporary times will be founded on the study of the text, and such an interpretation will constantly submit its presuppositions to verification by the text.

[II,B,1] The literal sense of Scripture is that which has been expressed directly by the inspired human authors. . . .

One branch of modern hermeneutics has stressed that human speech gains an altogether fresh status when put in writing. A written text has the capacity to be placed in new circumstances, which will illuminate it in different ways, adding new meanings to the original sense. . . . The literal sense is, from the start, open to further developments, which are produced through the "rereading" (*relectures*) of texts in new contexts.

It does not follow from this that we can attribute to a biblical text whatever meaning we like, interpreting it in a wholly subjective way. On the contrary, one must reject as inauthentic every interpretation alien to the meaning expressed by the human authors in their written text. To admit the possibility of such alien meanings would be equivalent to cutting off the biblical message from its root, which is the word of God in its historical communication; it would also mean opening the door to interpretations of a wildly subjective nature.

CHARACTERISTICS OF CATHOLIC INTERPRETATION

[III] Catholic exegesis freely makes use of the scientific methods and approaches that allow a better grasp of the meaning of texts in their linguistic, literary, socio-cultural, religious and historical contexts, while explaining them as well through studying their sources and attending to the personality of each author (cf. *Divino Afflante Spiritu* [Ench. Bibl., 557]). Catholic exegesis actively contributes to the development of new methods and to the progress of research.

[III,A,3] Granted that the expression of faith, such as it is found in the Sacred Scripture acknowledged by all, has had to renew itself continually in order to meet new situations, which explains the "rereadings" of many of the biblical texts, the interpretation of the Bible should likewise involve an aspect of creativity; it also ought to confront new questions so as to respond to them out the Bible.

Granted that tensions can exist in the relationship between various texts of Sacred Scripture, interpretation must necessarily show a certain pluralism. No single interpretation can exhaust the meaning of the whole, which is a symphony of many voices. Thus the interpreter of one particular text has to avoid seeking to dominate at the expense of others.

Sacred Scripture is in dialogue with communities of believers: it has come from their traditions of faith. . . .

Dialogue with Scripture in its entirety, which means dialogue with the understanding of the faith prevailing in earlier times, must be matched by a dialogue with the generation of today. Such dialogue will mean establishing a relationship of continuity. It will also involve acknowledging differences. Hence, the interpretation of Scripture involves a work of sifting and setting aside; it stands in continuity with earlier exegetical traditions, many elements of which it preserves and makes its own; but in other matters it will go its own way, seeking to make further progress.

INTERPRETATION OF THE BIBLE IN THE LIFE OF THE CHURCH

[IV,A] [W]ithin the Bible itself . . . one can point to instances of actualization: very early texts have been reread in the light of new circumstances and applied to the contemporary situation of the people of God. The same basic conviction stimulates believing communities of today to continue the process of actualization.

[IV,A,1] Actualization . . . cannot mean manipulation of the text. It is not a matter of projecting novel opinions or ideologies upon biblical writings, but of sincerely seeking to discover what the text has to say at the present time.

[IV,A,2] Actualization presupposes a correct exegesis of the text, part of which is the determining of its *literal sense*. Persons engaged in the work of actualization who do not themselves have training in exegetical procedures should have recourse to good introductions to Scripture; this will ensure that their interpretation proceeds in the right direction.

[IV,A,3] Clearly to be rejected also is every attempt at actualization set in a direction contrary to evangelical justice and charity, such as, for example, the use of the Bible to justify racial segregation, anti-Semitism, or sexism whether on the part of men or women. Particular attention is necessary, according to the spirit of the Second Vatican Council (cf. *Nostra Aetate*, 4), to avoid absolutely any actualization of certain texts of the New Testament that could provoke or reinforce unfavorable attitudes to the Jewish people. The tragic events of the past must, on the contrary, impel all to keep unceasing in mind that, according to the New Testament, the Jews remain "beloved" of God, "since the gifts and calling of God are irrevocable" (Rom. 11:28-29).

[Conclusion] From what has been said in the course of this long account . . . the first conclusion that emerges is that biblical exegesis fulfills, in the Church and in the world, an *indispensable task*. To attempt to bypass it when seeking to understand the Bible would be to create an illusion and display lack of respect for the inspired Scripture.

The Jewish People and Their
Sacred Scriptures in the Christian Bible

2002

JEWS IN THE GOSPELS AND ACTS OF THE APOSTLES

70. The Gospels and Acts have a basic outlook on Jews that is extremely positive because they recognise that the Jews are a people chosen by God for the fulfilment of his plan of salvation. This divine choice finds its highest confirmation in the person of Jesus, son of a Jewish mother, born to be the Saviour of his people, one who fulfils his mission by announcing the Good News to his people, and by performing works of healing and liberation that culminate in his passion and resurrection. The attachment to Jesus of a great number of Jews, during his public life and after his resurrection, confirms this perspective, as does Jesus' choice of twelve Jews to share in his mission and continue his work.

The Good News, accepted wholeheartedly in the beginning by many Jews, met with opposition from the leaders, who were eventually followed by the greater part of the people. The result was that between Jewish and Christian communities a conflict situation arose that clearly left its mark on the redaction of the Gospels and Acts.

1. The Gospel According to Matthew

The relationship between the First Gospel and the Jewish world is extremely close. Many details in it show a great familiarity with the Scriptures, the traditions and the mentality of the Jewish milieu. More than Mark and Luke, Matthew stresses the Jewish origin of Jesus: the genealogy presents him as "son of David, son of Abraham" (Mt 1:1) and goes no further back. The etymology of Jesus' name is underlined: the child of Mary will bear this name "because it is he who will save *his people* from their sins" (1:21). Jesus' mission during his public life is limited "to the lost sheep of the house of Israel" (15:24), and he assigns the same limits to the mission of the Twelve (10:5-6). More than the other evangelists, Matthew often takes care to

Pontifical Biblical Commission. *The Jewish People and Their Sacred Scriptures in the Christian Bible.* nos. 70-78, 86-87. Vatican City: Libreria Editrice Vaticana, 2002; Boston: Pauline Books & Media.

note that events in Jesus' life happened "so that what had been spoken through the prophets might be fulfilled" (2:23). Jesus himself makes it clear that he has come not to abolish the Law, but to fulfil it (5:17).

Nevertheless, it is clear that the Christian communities kept their distance from the Jewish communities that did not believe in Jesus Christ. A significant detail: Matthew does not say that Jesus taught "in *the* synagogues," but "in *their* synagogues" (4:23; 9:35; 13:54), in this way noting the separation. Matthew introduces two of the three Jewish parties described by the historian Josephus, the Pharisees and the Sadduccees, but always in a context of opposition to Jesus. This is also true for the scribes,[313] who are frequently associated with the Pharisees. Another significant fact: it is in the first prediction of the passion (16:21) that the three divisions of the Sanhedrin, "the elders, chief priests and scribes," make their first appearance together in the Gospel. They are also set in a situation of radical opposition to Jesus.

Jesus many times confronts the opposition of the scribes and Pharisees, and finally responds by a vigorous counter-offensive (23:2-7, 13-36) where the phrase "Scribes and Pharisees, hypocrites!" occurs six times. This invective certainly reflects, in part at least, the situation of Matthew's community. The redactional context is that of two groups living in close contact with one another: Jewish Christians, convinced that they belong to authentic Judaism, and those Jews who do not believe in Christ Jesus, considered by Christians to be unfaithful to their Jewish vocation in their docility to blind and hypocritical guides.

It should be noted that Matthew's polemic does not include Jews in general. These are not named apart from the expression "the King of the Jews," applied to Jesus (2:2; 27:11, 29, 37) and in the final chapter (28:15), a phrase of minor importance. The polemic is for the most part internal, between two groups both belonging to Judaism. On the other hand, only the leaders are in view. Although in Isaiah's message the whole vine is reprimanded (Is 5:1-7), in Matthew's parable it is only the tenants who are accused (Mt 21:33-41). The invective and the accusations hurled at the scribes and Pharisees are similar to those found in the prophets, and correspond to a contemporary literary genre which was common in Judaism (for example, Qumran) and also in Hellenism. Moreover, they put Christians themselves on guard against attitudes incompatible with the Gospel (23:8-12).

Furthermore, the anti-Pharisee virulence of Mt 23 must be seen in the context of the apocalyptic discourse of Mt 24-25. Apocalyptic language is employed in times of persecution to strengthen the capacity for resistance on the part of the persecuted minority, and to reinforce their hopes of a liberating divine intervention. Seen in this perspective, the vigour of the polemic is less astonishing.

Nevertheless, it must be recognised that Matthew does not always confine his polemics to the leading class. The diatribe of Mt 23 against the scribes and Pharisees is followed by an apostrophe addressed to Jerusalem. It is the whole city that is accused of "killing the prophets" and of "stoning those sent to it" (23:37), and it is for the whole city that punishment is predicted (23:38). Of its magnificent Temple "there will not remain a stone upon a stone" (24:2). Here is a situation parallel to Jeremiah's time (Jr 7:26). The prophet announced the destruction of the Temple and the ruin of the city (26:6,11). Jerusalem is about to become "a curse for all the nations of the earth" (26:6), exactly the opposite of the blessing promised to Abraham and his descendants (Gn 12:3; 22:18).

71. At the time of the Gospel's redaction, the greater part of the Jewish population had followed their leaders in their refusal to believe in Christ Jesus. Jewish Christians were only a minority. The evangelist, therefore, foresees that Jesus' threats were about to be fulfilled. These threats were not directed at Jews as Jews, but only insofar as they were in solidarity with their leaders in their lack of docility to God. Matthew expresses this solidarity in the passion narrative when he reports that at the instigation of the chief priests and elders "the crowd" demands of Pilate that Jesus be crucified (Mt 27:20-23). In response to the Roman governor's denial of responsibility, "all the people" present themselves took responsibility for putting Jesus to death (27:24-25). On the people's side, adopting this position certainly showed their conviction that Jesus merited death, but to the evangelist, such conviction was unjustifiable: the blood of Jesus was "innocent blood" (27:4), as even Judas recognised. Jesus would have made his own the words of Jeremiah: "Know for certain that if you put me to death, you will be bringing innocent blood upon yourselves and upon this city and its inhabitants" (Jr 26:15). From an Old Testament perspective, the sins of the leaders inevitably bring disastrous consequences for the whole community. If the Gospel was redacted after 70 AD, the evangelist knew that, like Jeremiah's prediction, Jesus' prediction had also been fulfilled. But he did not see this fulfilment as final, for all the Scriptures

attest that after the divine sanction God always opens up a positive perspective.[314] The discourse of Mt 23 does end on a positive note. A day will come when Jerusalem will say: "Blessed is he who comes in the name of the Lord" (23:39). Jesus' passion itself opens up the most positive perspective of all, for, from his "innocent blood" criminally shed, Jesus has constituted a "blood of the covenant," "poured out for the remission of sins" (26:38).

Like the people's cry in the passion narrative (27:25), the ending of the parable of the tenants seems to indicate that, at the time of the Gospel's composition, the majority of the Jews had followed their leaders in their refusal to believe in Jesus. Indeed, having predicted that "the kingdom of God will be taken away from you," Jesus did not add that the kingdom would be given "to other leaders," but would be given "to a *nation* producing its fruits" (21:43). The expression "a nation" is implicitly opposed to the "people of Israel"; this assuredly suggests that a great number of the subjects will not be of Jewish origin. The presence of Jews is in no way excluded, for the Gospel community is aware that this "nation" will be set up under the authority of the Twelve, in particular of Peter, and the Twelve are Jews. With these and other Jews "many will come from east and west and will eat with Abraham and Isaac and Jacob in the kingdom of heaven, while the heirs of the kingdom will be thrown into outer darkness" (8:11-12). This universal outlook is definitively confirmed at the end of the Gospel, for the risen Jesus commands the "eleven disciples" to go and teach "all the nations" (28:19). This ending, at the same time, confirms the vocation of Israel, for Jesus is a son of Israel and in him the prophecy of Daniel concerning Israel's role in history is fulfilled. The words of the risen One: "All authority in heaven and on earth has been given to me"[315] make explicit in what sense the universal vision of Daniel and the other prophets are henceforth to be understood.

Conclusion. More than the other Synoptic Gospels, Matthew is the Gospel of fulfilment—Jesus has not come to abolish, but to fulfil—for it insists more on the continuity with the Old Testament, basic for the idea of fulfilment. It is this aspect that makes possible the establishment of fraternal bonds between Christians and Jews. But on the other hand, the Gospel of Matthew reflects a situation of tension and even opposition between the two communities. In it Jesus foresees that his disciples will be flogged in the synagogues and pursued from town to town (23:34). Matthew therefore is concerned to provide for the Christians' defence. Since that situation has radically changed, Matthew's polemic need no longer interfere with relations between Christians and Jews, and the aspect of continuity can and ought to prevail. It is equally necessary to say this in relation to the destruction of the city and the Temple. This downfall is an event of the past which henceforth ought to evoke only deep compassion. Christians must be absolutely on their guard against extending responsibility for it to subsequent generations of Jews, and they must remind themselves that after a divine sanction, God never fails to open up positive new perspectives.

2. The Gospel According to Mark

72. Mark's Gospel is a message of salvation that does not inform us as to who the recipients are. The ending which has been added addresses it boldly "to the whole of creation," "into the whole world" (16:15), an address which corresponds to its universalist openness. As regards the Jewish people, Mark, himself a Jew, does not pass any judgement on them. The negative judgement of Isaiah (29:13) is applied in Mark only to the Pharisees and scribes (Mk 7:5-7). Apart from the title "King of the Jews" which is applied to Jesus five times in the passion narrative,[316] the title "Jew" appears only once in the Gospel, in the course of explaining Jewish customs (7:3), addressed obviously to non-Jews. This explanation comes in an episode in which Jesus criticises the Pharisees' extreme attachment to "the tradition of the elders," causing them to neglect "the commandments of God" (7:8). Mark mentions "Israel" only twice,[317] and twice also "the people."[318] In contrast, he frequently mentions "the crowd," for the most part certainly composed of Jews, and favourably disposed towards Jesus,[319] except in one passion episode, where the chief priests pressure them to choose Barabbas (15:11).

It is towards the religious and political authorities that Mark takes a critical stance. His criticism is essentially of their lack of openness to the salvific mission of Jesus: the scribes accuse Jesus of blasphemy, because he uses his power to forgive sins (2:7-10); they do not accept that Jesus "eats with publicans and sinners" (2:15-16); they say he is possessed by a devil (3:22). Jesus has continually to face opposition from them and from the Pharisees.[320]

The political authorities are less frequently called in question: Herod for the death of John the Baptist (6:17-28) and for his "leaven," juxtaposed with that of the Pharisees (8:15), the Jewish Sanhedrin, a political-religious authority (14:55; 15:1), and Pilate (15:15) for their role in the Passion.

In the *passion narrative*, the second Gospel attempts to reply to two questions: By whom is Jesus condemned and why is he put to death? It begins by giving a general answer that puts events in a divine light: all this happened "so that the Scriptures might be fulfilled" (14:49). It then reveals the role of the Jewish authorities and that of the Roman governor.

Jesus was arrested on the orders of the three components of the Sanhedrin, "chief priests, scribes and elders" (14:43). The arrest was the end result of a long process, set in motion in Mk 3:6, where, however, the protagonists are different: there they are the Pharisees who have joined the Herodians to plot against Jesus. A significant fact: it is in the first prediction of the passion that "the elders, chief priests and scribes" appear together for the first time (8:31). In 11:18 "the chief priests and the scribes" search for a way to eliminate Jesus. The three categories meet in 11:27, to put Jesus through an interrogation. Jesus recounts for them the parable of the murderous tenants; their reaction is "to look for a way to arrest him" (12:12). In 14:1, their intention is to apprehend him and "to put him to death." The betrayal of Jesus offers them a suitable opportunity (14:10-11). The arrest, followed by condemnation and death, is therefore the work of the nation's ruling class at that time. Mark regularly opposes the attitude of the leaders to that of "the crowd" or "the people," who are favourably disposed to Jesus. Three times the evangelist notes that in their attempts[321] to have Jesus killed, the authorities were inhibited by fear of the people's reaction. Nevertheless, at the end of the trial before Pilate, the chief priests succeeded in sufficiently inciting the attendant crowd to make them choose Barabbas (15:11) in preference to Jesus (15:13). The final decision of Pilate, powerless to calm the crowd, is to "satisfy" them, which, for Jesus, means crucifixion (15:15). This merely incidental crowd certainly cannot be confused with the Jewish people of that time, and even less with the Jews of every age. It should be said that they represent rather the sinful world (Mk 14:41) of which we are all a part.

It is the Sanhedrin that Mark holds guilty of having "condemned" Jesus (10:33; 14:64). About Pilate, Mark declines to say he condemned Jesus, but that, having no reason to accuse him (15:14), he handed him over to be put to death (15:15), something that makes Pilate even more culpable. The reason for the Sanhedrin's condemnation is that Jesus had uttered a "blasphemy" in his affirmative and circumstantial response to the High Priest's question whether he was "the Christ, the Son of the Blessed One" (14:61-64). In this way Mark reveals the most dramatic point of rupture between the Jewish authorities and the person of Christ, a matter that continues to be the most serious point of division between Judaism and Christianity. For Christians, Jesus' response is not blasphemy, but the very truth manifested as such by his resurrection. To the Jewish community, Christians are wrong to affirm the divine sonship of Christ in a way that gives grave offence to God. However painful it be, this fundamental disagreement must not degenerate into mutual hostility, or allow the existence of a rich common patrimony to be forgotten, a heritage which includes faith in the one God.

Conclusion. Any interpretation of Mark's Gospel that attempts to pin responsibility for Jesus' death on the Jewish people, is erroneous. Such an interpretation, which has had disastrous consequences throughout history, does not correspond at all to the evangelist's perspective, which, as we have said, repeatedly opposes the attitude of the people or the crowd to that of the authorities hostile to Jesus. Furthermore, it is forgotten that the disciples were also part of the Jewish people. It is a question then of an improper transfer of responsibility, of the sort that is often encountered in human history.[322]

Rather, it is well to recall that the passion of Jesus is part of God's mysterious plan, a plan of salvation, for Jesus came "to serve and to give his life as a ransom for many" (10:45), and has made of the blood that he shed a "blood of the covenant" (14:24).

3. The Gospel According to Luke and the Acts of the Apostles

73. Addressed to the "most excellent Theophilus" to complete his Christian instruction (Lk 1:3-4; Ac 1:1), the Gospel of Luke and the book of Acts are writings very open to universalism and, at the same time, very well disposed towards Israel.

The Names "Israel," "the Jews," "the People"

The positive attitude to "Israel" is seen immediately in the infancy narratives, where the name appears seven times. It is found only five times in the rest of the Gospel, in much less positive contexts. The name of the Jews appears only five times, three of which occur in the title "King of the Jews" given to Jesus in the passion narrative. More significant is the use of the word "people" which occurs thirty-six times in the Gospel (as against twice in Mark's Gospel), usually in a favourable light, even at the end of the Passion narrative.[323]

In Acts, there is a positive outlook from the beginning, because the apostles announce the resurrection of Christ and the forgiveness of sins for "the whole house of Israel" (2:36), and they attract numerous followers (2:41; 4:4). The name Israel occurs fourteen times in the first part of Acts (Ac 1:6-13:24), and a fifteenth time at the end (28:20). With forty eight occurances the word "people" is much more frequent; "the people" are well disposed at first to the Christian community (2:47; 5:26), in the end they follow is the example of their leaders and turn hostile towards it (12:4, 11), to the extent of seeking the death of Paul, in particular (21:30-31). Paul insists on saying that he "has done nothing against the people" (28:17). The same evolution is reflected in the use of the word "Jews" (seventy-nine times). On the day of Pentecost (2:5), the Jews whom Peter addresses and respectfully calls by that name (2:14), are summoned to faith in the risen Christ and adhere to him in great numbers. At the start, the Word is addressed exclusively to them (11:19). But very quickly, especially after Stephen's martyrdom, they become persecutors. The putting to death of James by Herod Antipas was an event that pleased them (12:2-3), and their "anticipation" was that the same fate could be waiting for Peter (12:11). Before his conversion, Paul was a relentless persecutor (8:3; cf. Ga 1:13); but after conversion, from persecutor he became the persecuted: already at Damascus "the Jews plotted to kill him" (9:23). Nevertheless, Paul continues to preach Christ "in the synagogues of the Jews" (13:5; 14:1) and brings to the faith "a great multitude of Jews and Greeks" (14:1), but this success provokes the hostile reaction of the "unbelieving Jews" (14:2). The same treatment is frequently repeated, in various ways, right up to Paul's arrest in Jerusalem, incited by "the Jews of the province of Asia" (21:27). But Paul continues to proclaim with pride: "I am a Jew" (22:3). He suffers the hostility of the Jews, but does not reciprocate.

The Gospel Narrative

74. The infancy narrative creates an atmosphere very favourably disposed to the Jewish people. The announcements of extraordinary births reveal "Israel" (1:68) and "Jerusalem" (2:38) as beneficiaries of salvation in fulfilment of an economy rooted in the people's history. The result is "a great joy for all the people" (2:10), "redemption" (1:68-69), "salvation" (2:30-31), "glory for your people" (2:32). This good news is well received. But a future negative reaction to God's gift is glimpsed, for Simeon predicts to Mary that her Son will become a "sign of contradiction" and foretells that "a fall" will precede "the rising up" (or: the resurrection) "of many in Israel" (2:34). Thus he opens up a deep perspective in which the Saviour is at grips with hostile forces. A touch of universalism, inspired by Second Isaiah (42:6; 49:6), joins the "light of revelation to the nations" to the "glory of your people Israel" (2:32), a conjoining which clearly shows that universalism does not mean being anti-Jewish.

In the rest of the Gospel, Luke inserts further touches of universalism: first in relation to the preaching of John the Baptist (3:6; cf. Is 40:5), and then by tracing the genealogy of Jesus back to Adam (3:38). However, the first episode of Jesus' ministry at Nazareth at once shows that universalism will create problems. Jesus appeals to his fellow townspeople to renounce a possessive attitude to his miracles and accept that these gifts are also for the benefit of foreigners (4:23-27). Their resentful reaction is violent: rejection and attempted murder (4:28-29). Thus Luke clarifies in advance what the repeated reaction of Jews will be to Paul's success among the Gentiles. The Jews violently oppose a preaching that sweeps away their privileges as the chosen people.[324] Instead of opening out to the universalism of Second Isaiah, they follow Baruch's counsel not to share their privileges with strangers (Ba 4:3). Other Jews resist that temptation and generously give themselves to the service of evangelisation (Ac 18:24-26).

Luke reports gospel traditions depicting Jesus in conflict with the scribes and Pharisees (Lk 5:17–6:11). In 6:11, however, he plays down the hostility of those adversaries by not attributing to them a murderous intention from the beginning, unlike Mk 3:6. Luke's polemical discourse against the Pharisees (11:42-44), later extended to include the "lawyers" (11:46-52) is considerably shorter than Mt 23:2-39. The parable of the Good Samaritan is an instruction on the universality of love in reply to a lawyer's question (Lk 10:29, 36-37). This puts the Jewish priest and Levite in a bad light, while proposing a Samaritan as a model (cf. also 17:12-19). The parables of mercy (15:4-32), addressed to the Pharisees and scribes, also urge an openness of heart. The parable of the merciful father (15:11-32) who invites the elder son to open his heart to the prodigal, does not directly apply to relations between Jews and Gentiles, although this application is often made (the elder son represents observant Jews who are less open to accepting pagans whom they consider to be sinners). Luke's larger context, nevertheless, makes this application possible because of his insistence on universalism.

The parable of the coins (19:11-27) has some very significant special features. There is the pretender to royalty who suffers hostility from his fellow citizens. He must go to a foreign country to be invested with royal power. On his return, he has his opponents executed. This parable, together with that of the murderous vineyard tenants (20:9-19), is a warning by Jesus of the consequences of rejecting him. Other passages in Luke's Gospel expressing Jesus' pain at the prospect of these tragic consequences, complete the picture: he weeps over Jerusalem (19:41-44) and he disregards his own sufferings to concentrate on the misfortune of the women and children of that city (23:28-31).

Luke's passion narrative is not particularly severe on the Jewish authorities. During Jesus' appearance before "the assembly of the elders of the people, chief priests and scribes" (22:66-71), Luke spares Jesus from confrontation with the High Priest, the accusation of blasphemy and condemnation, all of which serve to play down the culpability of Jesus' enemies. They bring accusations of a political order before Pilate (23:2). Pilate declares three times that Jesus is innocent (23:4, 14, 22), but intends to "give him a lesson" (23:16, 22) by having him flogged, and finally succumbs to the growing pressure of the mob (23:23-25) that includes "chief priests, leaders of the people" (23:13). In the events that follow, the "leaders" remain hostile (23:35), while the people are more favourably disposed towards Jesus (23:27, 45, 48), just as they were during his public life, as we have already noted. Jesus prays for his executioners whom he generously excuses, "for they do not know what they are doing" (23:34).

In the name of the *risen* Jesus "repentance and forgiveness of sins" is to be "proclaimed to all the nations" (24:47). This universalism has no polemical connotation, for the phrase emphasises that this preaching must "begin from Jerusalem." The perspective corresponds to Simeon's vision of messianic salvation, prepared by God as "a light of revelation to the Gentiles and for glory to your people Israel" (2:30-32).

Therefore, what the Third Gospel transmits to Acts is then substantially favourable to the Jewish people. The forces of evil have had their "hour." "Chief priests, captains of the Temple guard and elders" have been their instruments (22:52-53). But they have not prevailed. God's plan is fulfilled in accordance with the Scriptures (24:25-27,44-47), and it is a merciful plan for the salvation of all.

The Acts of the Apostles

75. The beginning of Acts depicts Christ's apostles passing from a narrow perspective, the establishment of the kingdom for Israel (Ac 1:6), to a universal one of witness "to the ends of the earth" (1:8). The Pentecost episode, curiously enough, sympathetically places Jews in this universal perspective: "There were devout Jews from every nation under heaven living in Jerusalem" (2:5). These Jews are the first recipients of the apostolic preaching, symbolising at the same time the universal destination of the Gospel. Luke suggests as well, more than once, that far from being mutually exclusive, Judaism and universalism go together.

The kerygmatic or missionary discourses preach the mystery of Jesus by emphasising the strong contrast between the human cruelty which put Jesus to death and the liberating intervention of God who raised him up. "Israel's" sin was to have "put to death the Prince of Life" (3:15). This sin, which is principally that of the "leaders of the people" (4:8-10) or the "Sanhedrin" (5:27-30), is recalled only as a basis for an appeal to conversion and faith. Besides, Peter attenuates the culpability, not only of the "Israelites" but even of their "leaders" by saying that they acted "out of ignorance" (3:17). Such forbearance is impressive. It corresponds to the teaching and attitude of Jesus (Lk 6:36-37; 23:34).

Nevertheless, the Christian preaching quickly stirs up opposition on the part of the Jewish authorities. The Sadduccees oppose the apostles' "proclaiming that in Jesus there is the resurrection of the dead" (Ac 4:2) in which they do not believe (Lk 20:27). But a very influential Pharisee, Gamaliel, takes the side of the apostles in thinking that their enterprise possibly "comes from

God" (Ac 5:39). Then opposition decreases for a while. It flares up again in Hellenistic synagogues when Stephen, himself a Hellenistic Jew, works "great wonders and signs among the people" (6:8-15). At the end of his discourse before members of the Sanhedrin, Stephen has recourse to the invective of the prophets (7:51). He is stoned. Following Jesus' example, he prays to the Lord that "this sin be not held against them" (7:60; cf. Lk 23:34). "That day a severe persecution began against the Church in Jerusalem" (Ac 8:1). "Saul" zealously took part in it (8:3; 9:13).

After his conversion and during all his missionary journeys, he himself—as we have already noted—experiences the opposition of his fellow countrymen, sparked by the success of his universalist preaching. This is particularly evident immediately after his arrest in Jerusalem. When he spoke "in the Hebrew language," "the assembly of people" (21:36) first heard him calmly (22:2), but from the moment he mentions his being sent "to the nations," they get terribly agitated and demand his death (22:21-22).

Acts ends on a surprising, but all the more significant, note. Shortly after his arrival in Rome, Paul "called together the local leaders of the Jews" (28:17), a unique gesture. He wants "to convince them about Jesus both from the Law of Moses and the prophets" (28:23). What he wished to obtain was not individual adherents, but a collective decision involving the whole Jewish community. After his unsuccessful attempt, he repeats the very harsh words of Isaiah concerning the hardness of "this people" (28:25-27; Is 6:9-10), and announces instead the docile acceptance that the nations will give to the salvation offered by God (28:28). In this ending, which gives rise to interminable discussion, Luke apparently wishes to accept the undeniable fact that, in the end, the Jewish people collectively did not accept the Gospel of Christ. At the same time, Luke wishes to reply to an objection that could be made against the Christian faith, by showing that this situation had already been foreseen in the Scriptures.

Conclusion

In Luke's oeuvre, there is no doubt that there is a profound respect for the Jewish reality insofar as it has a primary role in the divine plan of salvation. Nevertheless, in the course of the narrative, tensions become obvious. Luke tones down the polemics encountered in the other Synoptics. But he is unable, it seems,—and does not wish—to hide the fact that Jesus suffered fierce opposition from the leaders of his people and that, as a result, the apostolic preaching finds itself in an analogous situation. If a sober recounting of this undeniable Jewish opposition amounts to anti-Judaism, then Luke could be accused of it. But it is obvious that this way of looking at it is to be rejected. Anti-Judaism consists rather of cursing and hating the persecutors, and their people as a whole. The Gospel message, on the contrary, invites Christians to bless those who curse them, to do good to those who hate them, and to pray for those who persecute them (Lk 6:27-28), following the example of Jesus (23:34) and of the first Christian martyr (Ac 7:60). This is one of the basic lessons of Luke's work. It is regrettable that in the course of the centuries following it has not been more faithfully followed.

4. The Gospel According to John

76. About the Jews, the Fourth Gospel has a very positive statement, made by Jesus himself in the dialogue with the Samaritan woman: "Salvation comes from the Jews" (Jn 4:22).[325] Elsewhere, to the statement of the High Priest Caiaphas who said that it was "advantageous" "to have one man die for the people," the evangelist sees a meaning in the word inspired by God and emphasises that "Jesus was about to die for the nation," adding "not for the nation only, but to gather into one the dispersed children of God" (Jn 11:49-52). The evangelist betrays a vast knowledge of Judaism, its feasts, its Scriptures. The value of the Jewish patrimony is clearly acknowledged: Abraham saw Jesus' day and was glad (8:56); the Law is a gift given through Moses as intermediary (1:17); "the Scripture cannot be annulled" (10:35); Jesus is the one "about whom Moses in the Law and also the prophets wrote" (1:45); he is "a Jew" (4:9) and "King of Israel" (1:49) or "King of the Jews" (19:19-22). There is no serious reason to doubt that the evangelist was Jewish and that the basic context for the composition of the Gospel was relations with the Jews.

The word "Jews" is found seventy-one times in the Fourth Gospel, usually in the plural, three times in the singular (3:25; 4:9; 18:35). It is applied especially to "Jesus" (4:9). The name "Israelite" only appears once; it is a title of honour (1:47). A certain number of Jews are well disposed to Jesus. One such is Nicodemus, a "leader of the Jews" (3:1) who saw Jesus as a teacher come from God (3:2), defends him before his Pharisee colleagues (7:50-51) and, after his death on the cross, takes charge of his burial (19:39). At the end, "many of the leaders" believed in Jesus, but lacked courage to declare themselves as his disciples (12:42). The evangelist frequently reports that "many" people came to believe in Jesus.[326] The context shows that it is the Jews, except in 4:39, 41; the evangelist is sometimes precise, though rarely sufficiently so (8:31; 11:45; 12:11).

Nonetheless, "the Jews" are often hostile to Jesus. Their opposition begins with the curing of the paralytic on the sabbath day (5:16). It intensifies when Jesus makes himself "equal to God"; they try from then on to have him put to death (5:18). Later, like the High Priest during the trial of Jesus in Mt 26:65 and Mk 14:64, they accuse him of "blasphemy" and try to punish him accordingly by stoning (10:31-33). It has been noted with good reason that much of the Fourth Gospel anticipates the trial of Jesus and gives him the opportunity to defend himself and accuse his accusers. These are often called "the Jews" without further precision, with the result that an unfavourable judgement is associated with that name. But there is no question here of anti-Jewish sentiment, since—as we have already noted—the Gospel recognises that "salvation comes from the Jews" (4:22). This manner of speaking only reflects the clear separation that existed between the Christian and Jewish communities.

A more serious accusation made by Jesus against "the Jews" is that of having the devil for a father (8:44); it should be noted that this accusation is not made against the Jews insofar as they are Jews, but, on the contrary, insofar as they are not true Jews, since they entertain murderous intentions (8:37), inspired by the devil, who is "a murderer from the beginning" (8:44). The only concern here is a small number of Jesus' contemporaries, paradoxically, of "Jews who had believed in him" (8:31). By accusing them openly, the Fourth Gospel puts other Jews on guard against the temptation to similar murderous thoughts.

77. By translating "the Jews" as "the Judeans," an attempt has been made to eliminate the tensions that the Fourth Gospel can provoke between Christians and Jews. The contrast then would not be between the Jews and Jesus' disciples, but between the inhabitants of Judea, presented as hostile to Jesus, and those of Galilee, presented as flocking to their prophet. Contempt by Judeans for Galileans is certainly expressed in the Gospel (7:52), but the evangelist did not draw the lines of demarcation between faith and refusal to believe along geographical lines, he distinguishes Galilean Jews who reject Jesus' teaching as *hoi Ioudaioi* (6:41, 52).

Another interpretation of "the Jews" identifies them with "the world" based on affirmations which express a comparison (8:23) or parallelism between them.[327] But the world of sinners, by all accounts, extends beyond Jews who are hostile to Jesus.

It has also been noted that in many Gospel passages "the Jews" referred to are the Jewish authorities (chief priests, members of the Sanhedrin) or sometimes the Pharisees. A comparison between 18:3 and 18:12 points in this direction. In the passion narrative, John frequently mentions "the Jews" where the Synoptics speak of Jewish authorities. But this observation holds good only for a certain restricted number of passages and such precision cannot be introduced into a translation of the Gospel without being unfaithful to the text. These are echoes of opposition to Christian communities, not only on the part of the Jewish authorities, but from the vast majority of Jews, in solidarity with their leaders (cf. Ac 28:22). Historically, it can be said that only a minority of Jews contemporaneous with Jesus were hostile to him, that a smaller number were responsible for handing him over to the Roman authorities; and that fewer still wanted him killed, undoubtedly for religious reasons that seemed important to them.[328] But these succeeded in provoking a general demonstration in favour of Barabbas and against Jesus,[329] which permitted the evangelist to use a general expression, anticipating a later evolution.

At times in the Gospel the separation of Jesus' disciples from "the Jews" is evident in the expulsion from the synagogue imposed on Jews who believed in Jesus.[330] It is possible that the Jews in the Johannine communities experienced this treatment, since they would be considered unfaithful to Jewish monotheistic faith (which, in fact, was not at all the case, since Jesus said: "I and the Father *are one*": 10:30). The result was that it became almost standard to use "the Jews" to designate those who kept this name for themselves alone, in their opposition to the Christian faith.

78. *Conclusion.* The ministry of Jesus stirred up the mounting opposition on the part of the Jewish authorities, who, finally, decided to hand Jesus over to the Roman authorities to have him put to death. But he arose alive to give true life to all who believe in him. The Fourth Gospel recalls these events,

and re-evaluates them in the light of the experience of the Johannine communities that had encountered opposition from the Jewish communities.

The actions and words of Jesus show that he had a very close filial relationship with God that was unique of its kind. The apostolic catechesis progressively deepened its understanding of this relationship. In the Johannine communities, there was an insistence on the close relationship between Son and Father and on the divinity of Jesus, who is "the Christ, the Son of God" (20:31) in a transcendent sense. This teaching provoked opposition from the synagogue leaders, followed by the whole Jewish community. Christians were expelled from the synagogues (16:2) and were exposed, at the same time, to harassment by the Roman authorities, since they no longer enjoyed the franchise granted to Jews.

The polemic escalated on both sides. The Jews accused Jesus of being a sinner (9:24), a blasphemer (10:33) and of having a devil.[331] Those who believed in him were considered ignorant or accursed (7:49). On the Christian side, Jews were accused of disobedience to God's word (5:38), resisting his love (5:42) and pursuing vainglory (5:44).

Christians, no longer able to participate in Jewish cultic life, became more aware of the plenitude they had received from the Word made flesh (1:16). The risen Christ is the source of living water (7:37-38), light of the world (8:12), bread of life (6:35), and new Temple (2:19-22). Having loved his own to the end (13:1), he gave them his new commandment of love (13:34). Everything must be done to stir up faith in him, and, through faith, life (20:31). In the Gospel, polemics are secondary. What is of the greatest importance is the revelation of the "gift of God" (4:10; 3:16), which is offered to all in Jesus Christ, especially to those "who have pierced him" (19:37).

5. Conclusion

The Gospels reveal that the fulfilment of God's plan necessarily brought with it a confrontation with evil, which must be eradicated from the human heart. This confrontation puts Jesus at odds with the leaders of his people, just like the ancient prophets. Already in the Old Testament, the people of God were seen under two antithetical aspects: on the one hand, as a people called to be perfectly united to God; and on the other, as a sinful people. These two aspects could not fail to manifest themselves during Jesus' ministry. During the Passion, the negative aspect seemed to prevail, even among the Twelve. But the resurrection showed that, in reality, the love of God was victorious and obtained for all the pardon of sin and a new life.

Notes

313. This observation is valid for the plural, not for the singular, in 8:19 and 13:52.

314. Is 8:23–9:6; Jer 31–32; Ezk 36:16-38.

315. Mt. 28:18; cf. Dn 7:14, 18, 27.

316. Mk 15:2, 9, 12, 18, 26.

317. Mk 12:29; 15:32.

318. Mk 7:6; 14:2.

319. Mk 11:18; 12:12; 14:2.

320. See also Mk 8:11-12, 15; 10:2-12; 11:27-33.

321. Mk 11:18; 12:12; 14:2.

322. This tendency continues to manifest itself: the responsibility of the Nazis has been extended to include all Germans, that of certain western lobbies to include all Europeans, that of certain illegal immigrants to include all Africans.

323. Luke notes that "a great multitude of people" followed Jesus (23:27), of whom the greater part were women "who beat their breasts and wailed for him" (23:27). After the crucifixion, "the people stood watching" (23:35); this watching prepares them for conversion: at the end when "all the people who had gathered to witness this sight and saw what took place, they beat their breasts and went away" (23:48).

324. Acts 13:44-45, 50; 14:2-6; 17:4-7, 13; 18:5-6.

325. See above II, B, 3(b), n. 32.

326. Jn 2:23; 4:39, 41; 7:31; 8:30-31; 10:42; 11:45; 12:11, 42.

327. Jn 1:10, 11; 15:18, 25.

328. Jn 5:18; 10:33; 19:7.

329. Jn 18:38-40; 19:14-15.

330. Jn 9:22; 12:42; 16:2.

331. Jn 7:20; 8:48, 51; 10:20.

PASTORAL ORIENTATIONS

86. The Second Vatican Council, in its recommendation that there be "understanding and mutual esteem" between Christians and Jews, declared that these will be "born especially from biblical and theological study, as well as from fraternal dialogue."[347] The present Document has been composed in this spirit; it hopes to make a positive contribution to it, and encourages in the Church of Christ the love towards Jews that Pope Paul VI emphasized on the day of the promulgation of the conciliar document *Nostra Aetate*.[348]

With this text, Vatican Two laid the foundations for a new understanding of our relations with Jews when it said that "according to the apostle (Paul), the Jews, because of their ancestors, still remain very dear to God, whose gifts and calling are irrevocable (Rm 11:29)."[349]

Through his teaching, John Paul II has, on many occasions, taken the initiative in developing this Declaration. During a visit to the synagogue of Mainz (1980) he said: "The encounter between the people of God of the Old Covenant, which has never been abrogated by God (cf. Rm 11:29), and that of the New Covenant is also an *internal* dialogue in our Church, similar to that between the first and second part of its Bible."[350] Later, addressing the Jewish communities of Italy during a visit to the synagogue of Rome (1986), he declared: "The Church of Christ discovers its 'links' with Judaism 'by pondering its own mystery' (cf. *Nostra Aetate*). The Jewish religion is not 'extrinsic' to us, but in a certain manner, it is 'intrinsic' to our religion. We have therefore a relationship with it which we do not have with any other religion. You are our favoured brothers and, in a certain sense, one can say our elder brothers."[351] Finally, in the course of a meeting on the roots of anti-Jewish feeling among Christians (1997) he said: "This people has been called and led by God, Creator of heaven and earth. Their existence then is not a mere natural or cultural happening, . . . It is a supernatural one. This people continues in spite of everything to be the people of the covenant and, despite human infidelity, the Lord is faithful to his covenant."[352] This teaching was given the stamp of approval by John Paul II's visit to Israel, in the course of which he addressed Israel's Chief Rabbis in these terms: "We (Jews and Christians) must work together to build a future in which there will be no more anti-Jewish feeling among Christians, or any anti-Christian feeling among Jews. We have many things in common. We can do much for the sake of peace, for a more human and more fraternal world."[353]

On the part of Christians, the main condition for progress along these lines lies in avoiding a one-sided reading of biblical texts, both from the Old Testament and the New Testament, and making instead a better effort to appreciate the whole dynamism that animates them, which is precisely a dynamism of love. In the Old Testament, the plan of God is a union of love with his people, a paternal love, a spousal love and, notwithstanding Israel's infidelities, God will never renounce it, but affirms it in perpetuity (Is 54:8; Jr 31:3). In the New Testament, God's love overcomes the worst obstacles; even if they do not believe in his Son whom he sent as their Messiah Savior, Israelites are still "loved" (Rm 11:29). Whoever wishes to be united to God, must also love them.

87. The partial reading of texts frequently gives rise to difficulties affecting relations with the Jews. The Old Testament, as we have seen, is not sparing in its reproaches against Israelites, or even in its condemnations. It is very demanding towards them. Rather than casting stones at the Jews, it is better to see them as illustrating the saying of the Lord Jesus: "To whom much is given, from him much is expected" (Lk 12:48), and this saying applies to us Christians as well. Certain biblical narratives present aspects of disloyalty or cruelty which today would be morally inadmissible, but they must be understood in their historical and literary contexts. The slow historical progress of revelation must be recognized: the divine pedagogy has taken a group of people where it found them and led them patiently in the direction of an ideal union with God and towards a moral integrity which our modern society is still far from attaining. This education must avoid two opposite dangers, on the one hand, of attributing to ancient prescriptions an ongoing validity for Christians (for example, refusing blood transfusions on biblical grounds) and, on the other hand, of rejecting the whole Bible on the pretext of its cruelties. As regards ritual precepts, such as the rules for pure and impure, one has to be conscious of their symbolic and anthropological import, and be aware of their sociological and religious functions.

In the New Testament, the reproaches addressed to Jews are not as frequent or as virulent as the accusations against Jews in the Law and the Prophets. Therefore, they no longer serve as a basis for anti-Jewish sentiment. To use them for this purpose is contrary to the whole tenor of the New Testament.

Real anti-Jewish feeling, that is, an attitude of contempt, hostility and persecution of the Jews as Jews, is not found in any New Testament text and is incompatible with its teaching. What is found are reproaches addressed to certain categories of Jews for religious reasons, as well as polemical texts to defend the Christian apostolate against Jews who oppose it.

But it must be admitted that many of these passages are capable of providing a pretext for anti-Jewish sentiment and have in fact been used in this way. To avoid mistakes of this kind, it must be kept in mind that the New Testament polemical texts, even those expressed in general terms, have to do with concrete historical contexts and are never meant to be applied to Jews of all times and places merely because they are Jews. The tendency to speak in general terms, to accentuate the adversaries' negative side, and to pass over the positive in silence, failure to consider their motivations and their ultimate good faith, these are characteristics of all polemical language throughout antiquity, and are no less evident in Judaism and primitive Christianity against all kinds of dissidents.

The fact that the New Testament is essentially a proclamation of the fulfilment of God's plan in Jesus Christ, puts it in serious disagreement with the vast majority of the Jewish people who do not accept this fulfilment. The New Testament then expresses at one and the same time its attachment to Old Testament revelation and its disagreement with the Synagogue. This discord is not to be taken as "anti-Jewish sentiment," for it is disagreement at the level of faith, the source of religious controversy between two human groups that take their point of departure from the same Old Testament faith basis, but are in disagreement on how to conceive the final development of that faith. Although profound, such disagreement in no way implies reciprocal hostility. The example of Paul in Rm 9–11 shows that, on the contrary, an attitude of respect, esteem and love for the Jewish people is the only truly Christian attitude in a situation which is mysteriously part of the beneficent and positive plan of God. Dialogue is possible, since Jews and Christians share a rich common patrimony that unites them. It is greatly to be desired that prejudice and misunderstanding be gradually eliminated on both sides, in favour of a better understanding of the patrimony they share and to strengthen the links that bind them.

Notes

347. Declaration *"Nostra Aetate"* on relations of the Church with non-Christian religions, no 4.

348. Paul VI, homily of October 28th, 1965: *"ut erga eos reverentia et amor adhibeatur spesque in iis collocetur"*: ("that there be respect and love towards them and that hope is placed in them").

349. AAS 58 (1966) 740.

350. *Documentation Catholique* 77 (1980) 1148.

351. *Documentation Catholique* 83 (1986) 437.

352. *Documentation Catholique* 94 (1997) 1003.

353. *Documentation Catholique* 97 (2000) 372.

STATEMENTS OF POPE JOHN PAUL II

Address at the Great Synagogue of Rome

Pope John Paul II
April 13, 1986

4. Today's visit is meant to make a decisive contribution to the consolidation of the good relations between our two communities, in imitation of the example of so many men and women who have worked and who are still working today, on both sides, to overcome old prejudices and to secure ever wider and fuller recognition of that "bond" and that "common spiritual patrimony" that exists between Jews and Christians.

This is the hope expressed in the fourth paragraph of the Council's Declaration *Nostra Aetate*, which I have just mentioned, on the relationship of the Church to non-Christian religions. The decisive turning-point in relations between the Catholic Church and Judaism, and with individual Jews, was occasioned by this brief but incisive paragraph.

We are all aware that, among the riches of this paragraph no. 4 of *Nostra Aetate*, three points are especially relevant. I would like to underline them here, before you, in this truly unique circumstance.

The first is that the Church of Christ discovers her "bond" with Judaism by "searching into her own mystery" (cf. *Nostra Aetate*, ibid.). The Jewish religion is not "extrinsic" to us, but in a certain way is "intrinsic" to our own religion. With Judaism therefore we have a relationship which we do not have with any other religion. You are our dearly beloved brothers and, in a certain way, it could be said that you are our elder brothers.

The second point noted by the Council is that no ancestral or collective blame can be imputed to the Jews as a people for "what happened in Christ's passion" (cf. *Nostra Aetate*, ibid.). Not indiscriminately to the Jews of that time, nor to those who came afterwards, nor to those of today. So any alleged theological justification for discriminatory measures or, worse

John Paul II. *Pope John Paul II on Jews and Judaism 1979-1986*, edited by Eugene J. Fisher and Leon Klenicki, no. 4. Washington, DC: United States Conference of Catholic Bishops, 1987.

still, for acts of persecution is unfounded. The Lord will judge each one "according to his own works," Jews and Christians alike (cf. Rom 2:6).

The third point that I would like to emphasize in the Council's Declaration is a consequence of the second. Notwithstanding the Church's awareness of her own identity, it is not lawful to say that the Jews are "repudiated or cursed," as if this were taught or could be deduced from the Sacred Scriptures of the Old or the New Testament (cf. *Nostra Aetate*, ibid.). Indeed, the Council had already said in this same text of *Nostra Aetate*, and also in the Dogmatic Constitution *Lumen Gentium*, no. 16, referring to Saint Paul in the Letter to the Romans (11:28-29), that the Jews are beloved of God, who has called them with an irrevocable calling.

Address to the Pontifical Biblical Commission

Pope John Paul II
April 11, 1997

1. Your Eminence, I cordially thank you for the sentiments you have just expressed in presenting to me the Pontifical Biblical Commission at the beginning of its mandate. I cordially greet the old and new members of the Commission attending the audience. I greet the "old" members with warm gratitude for the tasks already completed and the "new" members with special joy inspired by hope. I am pleased to have this opportunity to meet you all personally and to say again to each of you how much I appreciate the generosity with which you put your competence as exegetes at the service of the Word of God and the Church's Magisterium.

The theme you have begun to study at this plenary session is of enormous importance: it is, in fact, fundamental for a correct understanding of the mystery of Christ and Christian identity. I would first like to emphasize this usefulness, which we could call *ad intra*. It is also inevitably reflected in a usefulness, so to speak, ad extra since awareness of one's own identity determines the nature of one's relations with others. In this case it determines the nature of the relations between Christians and Jews.

2. Since the second century AD, the Church has been faced with the temptation to separate the New Testament completely from the Old, and to oppose one to the other, attributing to them two different origins. The Old Testament, according to Marcion, came from a god unworthy of the name because he was vindictive and bloodthirsty, while the New Testament revealed a God of reconciliation and generosity. The Church firmly rejected this error, reminding all that God's tenderness was already revealed in the Old Testament. Unfortunately, the Marcionite temptation is making its appearance again in our time. However what occurs most frequently is an ignorance of the deep ties linking the New Testament to the Old, an ignorance that gives some people the impression that Christians have nothing in common with Jews.

Pope John Paul II, "Old Testament essential to know Jesus," *L'Osservatore Romano*, April 23, 1997, nos. 1-5.

Centuries of reciprocal prejudice and opposition have created a deep divide which the Church is now endeavoring to bridge, spurred to do so by the Second Vatican Council's position. The new liturgical Lectionaries have given more space to Old Testament texts, and the *Catechism of the Catholic Church* has been concerned to draw constantly from the treasures of Sacred Scripture.

3. Actually, it is impossible fully to express the mystery of Christ without reference to the Old Testament. Jesus' human identity is determined on the basis of his bond with the people of Israel, with the dynasty of David and his descent from Abraham. And this does not mean only a physical belonging. By taking part in the synagogue celebrations where the Old Testament texts were read and commented on, Jesus also came humanly to know these texts; he nourished his mind and heart with them, using them then in prayer and as an inspiration for his actions.

Thus he became an authentic son of Israel, deeply rooted in his own people's long history. When he began to preach and teach, he drew abundantly from the treasure of Scripture, enriching this treasure with new inspirations and unexpected initiatives. These—let us note—did not aim at abolishing the old revelation but, on the contrary, at bringing it to its complete fulfillment. Jesus understood the increasing opposition he had to face on the way to Calvary in the light of the Old Testament, which revealed to him the destiny reserved for the prophets. He also knew from the Old Testament that in the end God's love always triumphs.

To deprive Christ of his relationship with the Old Testament is therefore to detach him from his roots and to empty his mystery of all meaning. Indeed, to be meaningful, the Incarnation had to be rooted in centuries of preparation. Christ would otherwise have been like a meteor that falls by chance to the earth and is devoid of any connection with human history.

4. From her origins, the Church has well understood that the Incarnation is rooted in history and, consequently, she has fully accepted Christ's insertion into the history of the People of Israel. She has regarded the Hebrew Scriptures as the perennially valid Word of God, addressed to her as well as to the children of Israel. It is of primary importance to preserve and renew this ecclesial awareness of the essential relationship to the Old Testament.

I am certain that your work will make an excellent contribution in this regard; I am delighted with it and deeply grateful to you.

You are called to help Christians have a good understanding of their identity, an identity that is defined first and foremost by faith in Christ, the Son of God. But this faith is separable from its relationship to the Old Testament, since it is faith in Christ who "died for our sins *according to the Scriptures*" and "was raised . . . *in accordance with the Scriptures*" (1 Cor 15:3-4). The Christian must know that by belonging to Christ he has become "Abraham's offspring" (Gal 3:29) and has been grafted onto a cultivated olive tree (cf. Rom 11:17-24), that is, included among the People of Israel, to "share the richness of the olive tree" (Rom 11:17). If he has this firm conviction, he can no longer allow for Jews as such to be despised, or worse, ill-treated.

5. In saying this I do not mean to disregard the fact that the New Testament preserves traces of obvious tension between the early Christian communities and some groups of non-Christian Jews. St. Paul himself testifies [to this tension] in his Letters that as a non-Christian Jew he had proudly persecuted the Church of God (cf. Gal 1:13; 1 Cor 15:9; Phil 3:6). These painful memories must be overcome in charity, in accordance with Christ's command. Exegesis must always seek to advance in this direction and thereby help to decrease tensions and clear up misunderstandings.

Precisely in the light of all this, the work that you have begun is highly important and deserves to be carried out with care and commitment. It involves certain difficult aspects and delicate points, but it is very promising and full of great hope. I trust it will be very fruitful for the glory of God. With this wish, I assure you of a constant remembrance in prayer and I cordially impart a special Apostolic Blessing to you all.

Statements of the Pontifical Commission for Religious Relations with the Jews

Guidelines and Suggestions for Implementing the Conciliar Declaration *Nostra Aetate*, No. 4

Vatican Commission for Religious Relations with the Jews
December 1, 1974

II. LITURGY

The existing links between the Christian liturgy and the Jewish liturgy will be borne in mind. The idea of a living community in the service of God, and in the service of men for the love of God, such as it is realized in the liturgy, is just as characteristic of the Jewish liturgy as it is of the Christian one. To improve Jewish-Christian relations, it is important to take cognizance of those common elements of the liturgical life (formulas, feasts, rites, etc.) in which the Bible holds an essential place.

An effort will be made to acquire a better understanding of whatever in the Old Testament retains its own perpetual value (cf. *Dei Verbum*, 14-15), since that has not been canceled by the later interpretation of the New Testament. Rather, the New Testament brings out the full meaning of the Old, while both Old and New illumine and explain each other (cf. ibid., 16). This is all the more important since liturgical reform is now bringing the text of the Old Testament ever more frequently to the attention of Christians.

When commenting on biblical texts, emphasis will be laid on the continuity of our faith with that of the earlier Covenant, in the perspective of the promises, without minimizing those elements of Christianity which are original. We believe that those promises were fulfilled with the first coming of Christ. But it is none the less true that we still await their perfect fulfillment in his glorious return at the end of time.

With respect to liturgical readings, care will be taken to see that homilies based on them will not distort their meaning, especially when it is a question of passages which seem to show the Jewish people as such in an unfavorable light. Efforts will be made so to instruct the Christian people that they will understand the true interpretation of all the texts and their meaning for the contemporary believer.

Commission for Religious Relations with the Jews, "Guidelines and Suggestions for Implementing the Conciliar Declaration 'Nostra Aetate' (No. 4)." See *http://www.vatican.va.roman_curia/pontifical_councils/chrstuni/sub-index/index-relations-jews.htm* (accessed January 27, 2004).

Commissions entrusted with the task of liturgical translation will pay particular attention to the way in which they express those phrases and passages which Christians, if not well informed, might misunderstand because of prejudice. Obviously, one cannot alter the text of the Bible. The point is that, with a version destined for liturgical use, there should be an overriding preoccupation to bring out explicitly the meaning of a text,[1] while taking scriptural studies into account.

The preceding remarks also apply to introductions to biblical readings, to the Prayer of the Faithful, and to commentaries printed in missals used by the laity.

III. TEACHING AND EDUCATION

Although there is still a great deal of work to be done, a better understanding of Judaism itself and its relationship to Christianity has been achieved in recent years thanks to the teaching of the Church, the study and research of scholars, and also to the beginning of dialogue. In this respect, the following facts deserve to be recalled:

- It is the same God, "inspirer and author of the books of both Testaments" (*Dei Verbum*, 16), who speaks both in the old and new Covenants.
- Judaism in the time of Christ and the Apostles was a complex reality, embracing many different trends, many spiritual, religious, social and cultural values.
- The Old Testament and the Jewish tradition founded upon it must not be set against the New Testament in such a way that the former seems to constitute a religion of only justice, fear and legalism, with no appeal to the love of God and neighbor (cf: Dt. 6:5; Lv. 19:18; Mt. 22:34-40).
- Jesus was born of the Jewish people, as were his Apostles and a large number of his first disciples. When he revealed himself as the Messiah and Son of God (Mt. 16:16), the bearer of the new Gospel message, he did so as the fulfillment and perfection of the earlier Revelation. And, although his teaching had a profoundly new character, Christ, nevertheless, in many instances, took his stand on the teaching of the Old Testament. The New Testament is profoundly marked by its relation to the Old. As the Second Vatican Council declared: "God, the inspirer and author of the books of

both Testaments, wisely arranged that the New Testament be hidden in the Old and the Old be made manifest in the New" (*Dei Verbum*, 16). Jesus also used teaching methods similar to those employed by the rabbis of his time.

- With regard to the trial and death of Jesus, the Council recalled that "what happened in his passion cannot be blamed upon all the Jews then living, without distinction, nor upon the Jews of today" (*Nostra Aetate*, 4).

- The history of Judaism did not end with the destruction of Jerusalem, but rather went on to develop a religious tradition. And, although we believe that the importance and meaning of that tradition was deeply affected by the coming of Christ, it is still nonetheless rich in religious values.

- With the prophets and the apostle Paul, "the Church awaits the day, known to God alone, on which all peoples will address the Lord in a single voice and 'serve him with one accord' (Soph. 3:9)" (*Nostra Aetate*, 4).

- Information concerning these questions is important at all levels of Christian instruction and education. Among sources of information, special attention should be paid to the following:
  —catechisms and religious textbooks;
  —history books;
  —the mass-media (press, radio, cinema, television).

The effective use of these means presupposes the thorough formation of instructors and educators in training schools, seminaries and universities.

Research into the problems bearing on Judaism and Jewish-Christian relations will be encouraged among specialists, particularly in the fields of exegesis, theology, history and sociology. Higher institutions of Catholic research, in association if possible with other similar Christian institutions and experts, are invited to contribute to the solution of such problems. Wherever possible, chairs of Jewish studies will be created, and collaboration with Jewish scholars encouraged.

Notes

1. Thus the formula "the Jews," in St. John, sometimes according to the context means "the leaders of the Jews," or "the adversaries of Jesus," terms which express better the thought of the evangelist and avoid appearing to arraign the Jewish people as such. Another example is the use of the words "pharisee" and "pharisaism" which have taken on a largely pejorative meaning.

Notes on the Correct Way to Present the Jews and Judaism in Preaching and Catechesis in the Roman Catholic Church

Vatican Commission for Religious Relations with the Jews
June 24, 1985

10. Furthermore, in underlining the eschatological dimension of Christianity we shall reach a greater awareness that the people of God of the Old and the New Testament are tending towards a like end in the future: the coming or return of the Messiah—even if they start from two different points of view. It is more clearly understood that the person of the Messiah is not only a point of division for the people of God but also a point of convergence (cf: *Sussidi per l'ecumenismo*, of the diocese of Rome, no. 140). Thus it can be said that Jews and Christians meet in a comparable hope, founded on the same promise made to Abraham (cf. Gn. 12:1-3; Heb. 6:13-18).

11. Attentive to the same God who has spoken, hanging on the same word, we have to witness to one same memory and one common hope in Him who is the master of history. We must also accept our responsibility to prepare the world for the coming of the Messiah by working together for social justice, respect for the rights of persons and nations and for social and international reconciliation. To this we are driven, Jews and Christians, by the command to love our neighbor, by a common hope for the Kingdom of God and by the great heritage of the Prophets. Transmitted soon enough by catechesis, such a conception would teach young Christians in a practical way to co-operate with Jews, going beyond simple dialogue (cf. *Guidelines*, IV).

III. JEWISH ROOTS OF CHRISTIANITY

1. Jesus was and always remained a Jew, his ministry was deliberately limited "to the lost sheep of the house of Israel" (Mt. 15:24). Jesus is fully a man of his time, and of his environment—the Jewish Palestinian one of the first century, the anxieties and hopes of which he shared. This cannot but underline both the reality of the Incarnation and the very meaning of the history of salvation, as it has been revealed in the Bible (cf. Rm. 1:34; Gal. 4:4-5).

Commission for Religious Relations with the Jews, "Notes on the Correct Way to Present the Jews and Judaism in Preaching and Catechesis in the Roman Catholic Church." See *http://www.vatican.va/roman_curia/pontifical_councils/chrstuni/sub-index/index-relations-jews.htm* (accessed January 27, 2004).

2. Jesus' relations with biblical law and its more or less traditional interpretations are undoubtedly complex and he showed great liberty towards it (cf. the "antitheses" of the Sermon on the Mount, Mt. 5:21-48, bearing in mind the exegetical difficulties; his attitude to rigorous observance of the Sabbath: Mk. 3:1-6, etc.).

But there is no doubt that he wished to submit himself to the law (cf. Gal 4:4), that he was circumcised and presented in the Temple like any Jew of his time (cf. Lk. 2:21, 22-24), that he was trained in the law's observance. He extolled respect for it (cf. Mt. 5:17-20) and invited obedience to it (cf. Mt. 8:4). The rhythm of his life was marked by observance of pilgrimages on great feasts, even from his infancy (cf. Lk. 2:41-50; Jn. 2:13; 7-10, etc.). The importance of the cycle of the Jewish feasts has been frequently underlined in the Gospel of John (cf. 2:13; 5:1; 7:2; 10:37; 10:22; 12:1; 13:1; 18:28; 19:42, etc.).

3. It should be noted also that Jesus often taught in the Synagogues (cf. Mt. 4:23; 9:35; Lk. 4:14-18; Jn. 18:20, etc.) and in the Temple (cf. Jn. 18:20, etc.), which he frequented as did the disciples even after the Resurrection (cf. Acts 2:46; 3:1; 21:26, etc.). He wished to put in the context of synagogue worship the proclamation of his Messiahship (cf. Lk. 4:16-21). But above all he wished to achieve the supreme act of the gift of himself in the setting of the domestic liturgy of the Passover, or at least of the paschal festivity (cf. Mk 14:1, 12 and parallels; Jn. 18:28). This also allows of a better understanding of the "memorial" character of the Eucharist.

4. Thus the Son of God is incarnate in a people and a human family (cf. Gal. 4:4; Rm. 9:5). This takes away nothing, quite the contrary, from the fact that he was born for all men (Jewish shepherds and pagan wise men are found at his crib: Lk. 2:8-20; Mt. 2:1-12) and died for all men (at the foot of the cross there are Jews, among them Mary and John: Jn. 19:25-27, and pagans like the centurion: Mk. 15:39 and parallels). Thus, he made two peoples one in his flesh (cf. Eph. 2:14-17). This explains why with the *Ecclesia ex gentibus* we have, in Palestine and elsewhere, an *Ecclesia ex circumcisione*, of which Eusebius for example speaks (*H.E.*, IV, 5).

5. His relations with the Pharisees were not always or wholly polemical. Of this there are many proofs:

- It is Pharisees who warn Jesus of the risks he is running (Lk. 13:31);
- Some Pharisees are praised ("the scribe" of Mk. 12:34);
- Jesus eats with Pharisees (Lk. 7:36; 14:1).

6. Jesus shares, with the majority of Palestinian Jews of that time, some pharisaic doctrines: the resurrection of the body; forms of piety, like alms-giving, prayer, fasting (cf. Mt. 6:1-18) and the liturgical practice of address-ing God as Father; the priority of the commandment to love God and our neighbor (cf. Mk. 12:28-34). This is so also with Paul (cf. Acts 23:8), who always considered his membership of the Pharisees as a title of honor (cf. Acts 23:6; 26:5; Ph 3:5).

7. Paul also, like Jesus himself, used methods of reading and interpreting Scripture and of teaching his disciples which were common to the Pharisees of their time. This applies to the use of parables in Jesus' ministry, as also to the method of Jesus and Paul of supporting a conclusion with a quotation from Scripture.

8. It is noteworthy too that the Pharisees are not mentioned in accounts of the Passion. Gamaliel (Acts 5:34-39) defends the apostles in a meeting of the Sanhedrin. An exclusively negative picture of the Pharisees is likely to be inaccurate and unjust (cf. *Guidelines*, note 1; cf. AAS, p. 76). If in the Gospel and elsewhere in the New Testament there are all sorts of unfavor-able references to the Pharisees, they should be seen against the back-ground of a complex and diversified movement. Criticisms of various types of Pharisees are moreover not lacking in rabbinical sources (cf. the *Babylonian Talmud* and the *Sotah* treatise, 22b, etc.). "Phariseeism" in the pejorative sense can be rife in any religion. It may also be stressed that, if Jesus shows himself severe towards the Pharisees, it is because he is closer to them than to other contemporary Jewish groups (cf. supra, 17).

9. All this should help us to understand better what St. Paul says (Rm. 11:16ff) about the "root" and the "branches." The Church and Christianity, for all their novelty, find their origin in the Jewish milieu of the first century of our era, and more deeply still in the "design of God" (*Nostra Aetate*, no. 4), realized in the Patriarchs, Moses and the Prophets, down to its consummation in Christ Jesus.

IV. THE JEWS IN THE NEW TESTAMENT

1. The *Guidelines* already say (no. 1) that "the formula 'the Jews' sometimes, according to the context, means 'the leaders of the Jews' or 'the adversaries of Jesus,' terms which express better the thought of the evangelist and avoid appearing to arraign the Jewish people as such."

An objective presentation of the role of the Jewish people in the New Testament should take account of these various facts:

A. The Gospels are the outcome of long and complicated editorial work. The dogmatic constitution *Dei Verbum*, following the Pontifical Biblical Commission's Instruction *Sancta Mater Ecclesia*, distinguished three stages: "The sacred authors wrote the four Gospels, selecting some things from the many which had been handed on by word of mouth or in writing, reducing some of them to a synthesis, explicating some things in view of the situation of their Churches, and preserving the form of proclamation, but always in such fashion that they told us the honest truth about Jesus" (no. 19).

Hence, it cannot be ruled out that some references hostile or less than favorable to the Jews have their historical context in conflicts between the nascent Church and the Jewish community. Certain controversies reflect Christian-Jewish relations long after the time of Jesus.

To establish this is of capital importance if we wish to bring out the meaning of certain Gospel texts for the Christians of today.

All this should be taken into account when preparing catechesis and homilies for the last weeks of Lent and Holy Week (cf. *Guidelines*, II, *Sussidi per l'ecumenismo nella diocesi di Roma*, 1982, 144b).

B. It is clear on the other hand that there were conflicts between Jesus and certain categories of Jews of his time, among them Pharisees, from the beginning of his ministry (cf. Mk. 2:1-11, 24; 3:6, etc.).

C. There is moreover the sad fact that the majority of the Jewish people and its authorities did not believe in Jesus—a fact not merely of history but of theological bearing, of which St. Paul tries hard to plumb the meaning (Rm. chap. 9-11).

D. This fact, accentuated as the Christian mission developed, especially among the pagans, led inevitably to a rupture between Judaism and the young Church, now irreducibly separated and divergent in faith, and this stage of affairs is reflected in the texts of the New Testament and particularly in the Gospels. There is no question of playing down or glossing over this rupture; that could only prejudice the identity of either side.

Nevertheless it certainly does not cancel the spiritual "bond" of which the Council speaks (*Nostra Aetate*, no. 4) and which we propose to dwell on here.

E. Reflecting on this in the light of Scripture, notably of the chapters cited from the epistle to the Romans, Christians should never forget that the faith is a free gift of God (cf. Rm. 9:12) and that we should never judge the consciences of others. St. Paul's exhortation "do not boast" in your attitude to "the root" (Rm. 11:18) has its full point here.

F. There is no putting the Jews who knew Jesus and did not believe in him, or those who opposed the preaching of the apostles, on the same plane with Jews who came after or those of today. If the responsibility of the former remains a mystery hidden with God (cf. Rm. 11:25), the latter are in an entirely different situation. Vatican II in the declaration on *Religious Liberty* teaches that "all men should be immune from coercion" in such wise that in matters religious no one is to be forced to act in a manner contrary to his own beliefs (no. 2). This is one of the bases—proclaimed by the Council— on which the Judaeo-Christian dialogue rests.

2. The delicate question of responsibility for the death of Christ must be looked at from the standpoint of the conciliar declaration *Nostra Aetate*, (no. 4) and of the *Guidelines and Suggestions* (part III): "What happened in (Christ's) passion cannot be blamed upon all the Jews then living without distinction nor upon the Jews of today," especially since "authorities of the Jews and those who followed their lead pressed for the death of Christ." Again, further on: "Christ in his boundless love freely underwent his passion and death because of the sins of all men, so that all might attain salvation" (*Nostra Aetate*, no. 4). The *Catechism* of the Council of Trent teaches that Christian sinners are more to blame for the death of Christ than those

few Jews who brought it about—they indeed "knew not what they did" (Lk. 23:34) and we know it only too well (Pars I, caput V, Quaest. XI). In the same way and for the same reason, "the Jews should not be presented as repudiated or cursed by God, as if such views followed from the holy Scriptures" (*Nostra Aetate*, no. 4), even though it is true that "the Church is the new people of God (ibid.)."

4. We Remember: A Reflection on the *Shoah*

The Pontifical Commission for Religious Relations with the Jews
March 16, 1998

POPE JOHN PAUL II'S INTRODUCTORY LETTER

To My Venerable Brother Cardinal Edward Idris Cassidy:

On numerous occasions during my Pontificate I have recalled with a sense of deep sorrow the sufferings of the Jewish people during the Second World War. The crime which has become known as the *Shoah* remains and indelible stain on the history of the century that is coming to a close.

As we prepare for the beginning of the Third Millennium of Christianity, the Church is aware that the joy of a Jubilee is above all the joy that is based on the forgiveness of sins and reconciliation with God and neighbor. Therefore she encourages her sons and daughters to purify their hearts, through repentance of past errors and infidelities. She calls them to place themselves humbly before the Lord and examine themselves on the responsibility which they too have for the evils of our time.

It is my fervent hope that the document: "We Remember: A Reflection on the *Shoah*," which the Commission for Religious Relations with the Jews has prepared under your direction, will indeed help to heal the wounds of past misunderstandings and injustices. May it enable memory to play its necessary part in the process of shaping a future in which the unspeakable iniquity of the *Shoah* will never again be possible. May the Lord of history guide the efforts of Catholics and Jews and all men and women of good will as they work together for a world of true respect for the life and dignity of every human being, for all have been created in the image and likeness of God.

From the Vatican, 12 March 1998.

—Joannes Paulus II

Commission for Religious Relations with the Jews, "Notes on the Correct Way to Present the Jews and Judaism in Preaching and Catechesis in the Roman Catholic Church." See *http://www.vatican.va/roman_curia/pontifical_councils/chrstuni/sub-index/index-relations-jews.htm* (accessed January 27, 2004).

II. WHAT WE MUST REMEMBER

While bearing their unique witness to the Holy One of Israel and to the *Torah*, the Jewish people have suffered much at different times and in many places. But the *Shoah* was certainly the worst suffering of all. The inhumanity with which the Jews were persecuted and massacred during this century is beyond the capacity of words to convey. All this was done to them for the sole reason that they were Jews.

The very magnitude of the crime raises many questions. Historians, sociologists, political philosophers, psychologists and theologians are all trying to learn more about the reality of the *Shoah* and its causes. Much scholarly study still remains to be done. But such an event cannot be fully measured by the ordinary criteria of historical research alone. It calls for a "moral and religious memory" and, particularly among Christians, a very serious reflection on what gave rise to it.

The fact that the *Shoah* took place in Europe, that is, in countries of long-standing Christian civilization, raises the question of the relation between the Nazi persecution and the attitudes down the centuries of Christians towards Jews.

V. LOOKING TOGETHER TO A COMMON FUTURE

Looking to the future of relations between Christians and Jews, in the first place we appeal to our Catholic brothers and sisters to renew the awareness of the Hebrew roots of their faith. We ask them to keep in kind that Jesus was a descendant of David; that the Virgin Mary and the Apostles belonged to the Jewish people; that the Church draws sustenance from the root of that good olive tree on to which have been grafted the wild olive branches of the Gentiles (Cf. Romans 11:17-24); that the Jews are our dearly beloved brothers, indeed in a certain sense they are "our elder brothers."[21]

At the end of this Millennium the Catholic Church desires to express her deep sorrow for the failures of her sons and daughters in every age. This is an act of repentance (teshuva), since, as members of the Church, we are linked to the sins as well as the merits of all her children. The Church approaches with deep respect and great compassion the experience of extermination, the Shoah, suffered by the Jewish people during World War II. It is not a matter of mere words, but indeed of binding commitment. *"We would risk causing the victims of the most atrocious deaths to die again if we do not have an ardent desire for justice, if we do not commit ourselves to ensure that evil does not prevail over good as it did for millions of children of the Jewish people . . . Humanity cannot permit all that to happen again."*[22]

We pray that our sorrow for the tragedy which the Jewish people has suffered in our century will lead to a new relationship with the Jewish people. We wish to turn awareness of past sins into a firm resolve to build a new future in which there will be no more anti-Judaism among Christians or anti-Christian sentiment among Jews, but rather a shared mutual respect, as befits those who adore the one Creator and Lord and have a common father in faith, Abraham.

Finally, we invite all men and women of good will to reflect deeply on the significance of the *Shoah*. The victims from their graves, and the survivors through the vivid testimony of what they have suffered, have become a loud voice calling the attention of all of humanity. To remember this terrible experience is to become fully conscious of the salutary warning it entails: the spoiled seeds of anti-Judaism and anti-Semitism must never again be allowed to take root in any human heart.

Notes

21. Pope John Paul II, *Speech at the Synagogue of Rome*, 13 April 1986, 4: AAS 78 (1986), 1120.

22. Pope John Paul II, *Address on the Occasion of a Commemoration of the Shoah*, 7 April 1994, 3: *Insegnamenti* 17/1, 1994, 897 and 893.

Statements of the
United States Conference of
Catholic Bishops

Guidelines for Catholic-Jewish Relations

Bishops' Committee for Ecumenical and Interreligious Affairs
National Conference of Catholic Bishops
March 1967

In its *Declaration on the Relationship of the Church to Non-Christian Religions* of 1965, the Second Vatican Council issued an historic statement on the Jews and summoned all Catholics to re-appraise their attitude toward and relationship with the Jewish people. The Statement was, in effect, a culminating point of initiatives and pronouncements of recent pontiffs and of numerous endeavors in the Church concerned with Catholic-Jewish harmony. [It was also the point of convergence of many insights opened by Pope Paul's Encyclical *Ecclesiam Suam* and the Council's Constitution on the Church and Decree on Ecumenism.]

The call of the Council to a fraternal encounter with Jews may be seen, [further,] as one of the more important fruits of the spirit of renewal generated by the council in its deliberations and decrees. [Was it not indeed the Council's response to Pope John XXIII's famous words in which he embraced the Jewish people: "I am Joseph your brother"? (Gen 45:4). More specifically,] the Council's call is an acknowledgement of the conflicts and tensions that have separated Christians and Jews through the centuries and of the Church's determination, as far as possible, to eliminate them. It serves both in word and action as a recognition of the manifold sufferings and injustices inflicted upon the Jewish people by Christians in our own times as well as in the past. [The Statement] speaks from the highest level of the Church's authority to serve notice that injustices directed against the Jews at any time from any source can never receive Catholic sanction or support.

The message of the Council's statement is clear. Recalling in moving terms the "spiritual bond that ties the people of the New Covenant to Abraham's stock," the Fathers of the council remind us of the special place Jews hold in the Christian perspective, for "now as before God holds them as most

Secretariat for Catholic-Jewish Relations, and Bishops' Committee on Ecumenical and Interreligious Affairs, National Conference of Catholic Bishops. *Guidelines for Catholic-Jewish Relations*, 1-2, and 6-7 (no. 10). Washington, D.C.: United States Conference of Catholic Bishops, 1985.

dear for the sake of the patriarchs; he has not withdrawn his gifts or calling." Jews, therefore, the Fathers caution, are not "to be presented as rejected or accursed by God, as if this followed from Holy Scripture." The Passion of Jesus, moreover, "cannot be attributed without distinction to all Jews then alive, nor can it be attributed to the Jews of today." The Church, the statement declares, "decries hatred, persecutions, displays of anti-Semitism directed against the Jews at any time and by anyone."

In light of these principles the Fathers enjoin that "all see to it that nothing is taught, either in catechetic work or in the preaching of the Word of God, that does not conform to the truth of the Gospel and the spirit of Christ." . . .

10. The following themes which, among others, are viewed by Christian and Jew[ish experts] as important issues affecting Christian-Jewish relations merit the attention and study of Catholic educators and scholars:

    a. Scholarly studies and education[al] efforts . . . to show the common historical, biblical, doctrinal and liturgical heritage shared by Catholics and Jews, as well as their differences. . . .

    b. As the statement requires, the presentation of the Crucifixion story . . . in such a way as not to implicate all Jews of Jesus' time or of today in a collective guilt for the crime. . . .

    c. In keeping with the [Statement's] strong repudiation of anti-Semitism, a frank and honest treatment . . . in our history books, courses and . . . curricula . . . of the history of Christian anti-Semitism.

    d. [A study of the life of Jesus] and of the primitive Church in the setting of the . . . religious, social and cultural [features] of Jewish [life] in the first century.

    e. An explicit rejection . . . of the historically inaccurate notion that Judaism of that time, especially . . . Pharisaism, was a decadent formalism and hypocrisy[, well exemplified by Jesus' enemies]. . . .

    f. [An acknowledgment by] Catholic scholars [of] the living and complex reality of Judaism after Christ . . . and the permanent election of [Israel], alluded to by St. Paul (Rom 9:29), and [incorporation of] the results into Catholic teaching.

g. [A full and precise explanation] of the use . . . of [the] expression "the Jews" by St. John and other New Testament references [which] appear to place all Jews in a negative light. (These expressions and references should be fully and precisely clarified in accordance with the intent of the . . . statement . . . that Jews are not to be "presented as rejected or accursed by God as if this followed from Holy Scripture.")

Statement on Catholic-Jewish Relations

National Conference of Catholic Bishops
1975

7. Recalling past centuries . . . invites a sobering evaluation of our progress and warns against becoming over-confident about an early end to remaining problems. Those were centuries replete with alienation, misunderstanding, and hostility between Jews and Christians. While we rejoice that there are signs that anti-Semitism is declining in our country, conscience compels us to confront with candor the unhappy record of Jewish sufferings, both past and present. We make our own the statement of *Nostra Aetate*, ". . . for the sake of her common patrimony with the Jews, the Church decries hatred, persecutions, displays of anti-Semitism staged against Jews at whatever time in history and by whomsoever" and we reaffirm with the new Vatican *Guidelines* that "the spiritual bonds and historical links binding the Church to Judaism condemn (as opposed to the very spirit of Christianity) all forms of anti-Semitism. . . ." We urge all in the Church who work in the area of education, whether in the seminary, the school, or the pulpit, not only to avoid any presentation that might tend to disparage Jews or Judaism but also to emphasize those aspects of our faith which bear witness to our common patrimony and our spiritual ties with Jews.

8. Much of the alienation between Christian and Jew found its origins in a certain anti-Judaic theology which over the centuries has led not only to social friction with Jews but often to their oppression. One of the most hopeful developments in our time, powerfully assisted by *Nostra Aetate*, has been the decline of the old anti-Judaism and the reformation of Christian theological expositions of Judaism along more constructive lines.

9. The first major step in this direction was the repudiation of the charge that Jews were and are collectively guilty of the death of Christ. *Nostra Aetate* and the new *Guidelines* have definitely laid to rest this myth which has caused so much suffering to the Jewish people. There remains, however, the continuing task of ensuring that nothing which in any way approaches the

United States Conference of Catholic Bishops. *Pastoral Letters of the United States Catholic Bishops*, Vol. 5, edited by Hugh J. Nolan, 121-123, nos. 7-13. Washington, D.C.: United States Catholic Conference, 1984.

notion of Jewish collective guilt should be found in any Catholic medium of expression or communication. Correctly viewed, the disappearance of the charge of collective guilt of Jews pertains as much to the purity of the Catholic faith as it does to the defense of Judaism.

10. The Council's rejection of this charge against Jews has been interpreted by some commentators as an "exoneration" of the Jewish people. Such a view of the matter still persists. The truth is that the Council acknowledged that the Jewish people never were, nor are they now, guilty of the death of Christ.

11. *Nostra Aetate* was a new beginning in Catholic-Jewish relations and, as with all beginnings, we are faced with the task of revising some traditional understandings and judgments. The brief suggestions of the Council document have been taken up by some theologians, but their implications for theological renewal have not yet been fully explored. We therefore make a few recommendations in line with two themes of the document: the Jewish origins of the Church and the thought of St. Paul.

12. Christians have not fully appreciated their Jewish roots. Early in Christian history, a de-Judaizing process dulled our awareness of our Jewish beginnings. The Jewishness of Jesus, of his mother, his disciples, of the primitive Church, was lost from view. That Jesus was called Rabbi; that he was born, lived, and died under the Law; that He and Peter and Paul worshipped in the Temple—these facts were blurred by the controversy that alienated Christians from the Synagogue. How Jewish the Church was toward the midpoint of the first century is dramatically reflected in the description of the "Council of Jerusalem" (Acts 15). The question at issue was whether Gentile converts to the Church had to be circumcised and observe the Mosaic Law? The obligation to obey the Law was held so firmly by the Jewish Christians of that time that miraculous visions accorded to Peter and Cornelius (Acts 10) were needed to vindicate the contrary contention that Gentile Christians were not so obliged. By the third century, however, a de-Judaizing process had set in which tended to undervalue the Jewish origins of the Church, a tendency that has surfaced from time to time in devious ways throughout Christian history. Some catechists, homilists, and teachers still convey little appreciation of the Jewishness of that heritage and rich spirituality which we derive from Abraham, Moses, the prophets, the psalmists, and other spiritual giants of the Hebrew Scriptures.

13. Most essential concepts in the Christian creed grew at first in Judaic soil. Uprooted from that soil, these basic concepts cannot be perfectly understood. It is for reasons such as these that *Nostra Aetate* recommends joint "theological and biblical studies" with Jews. The Vatican *Guidelines* of 1975 encourage Catholic specialists to engage in new research into the relations of Judaism and Christianity and to seek out "collaboration with Jewish scholars." The renewal of Christian faith is the issue here, for renewal always entails to some extent a return to one's origins.

God's Mercy Endures Forever: Guidelines on the Presentation of Jews and Judaism in Catholic Preaching

Bishops' Committee on the Liturgy
National Conference of Catholic Bishops
September 1988

HISTORICAL PERSPECTIVES AND CONTEMPORARY PROCLAMATION

5. The strongly Jewish character of Jesus' teaching and that of the primitive Church was culturally adapted by the growing Gentile majority and later blurred by controversies alienating Christianity from emerging rabbinic Judaism at the end of the first century. "By the third century, however, a de-Judaizing process had set in which tended to undervalue the Jewish origins of the Church, a tendency that has surfaced from time to time in devious ways throughout Christian history" (*Statement on Catholic-Jewish Relations*, no. 12).

6. This process has manifested itself in various ways in Christian history. In the second century, Marcion carried it to its absurd extreme, teaching a complete opposition between the Hebrew and Christian Scriptures and declaring that different Gods had inspired the two Testaments. Despite the Church's condemnation of Marcion's teachings, some Christians over the centuries continued to dichotomize the Bible into two mutually contradictory parts. They argued, for example, that the New Covenant "abrogated" or "superseded" the Old, and that the Sinai Covenant was discarded by God and replaced with another. The Second Vatican Council, in *Dei Verbum* and *Nostra Aetate*, rejected these theories of the relationship between the Scriptures. In a major address in 1980, Pope John Paul II linked the renewed understanding of Scripture with the Church's understanding of its relationship with the Jewish people, stating that the dialogue, as "the meeting between the people of God of the Old Covenant, never revoked by God, is at the same time a dialogue within our Church, that is

Bishops' Committee on the Liturgy, United States Conference of Catholic Bishops. *God's Mercy Endures Forever: Guidelines on the Presentation of Jews and Judaism in Catholic Preaching*, nos. 5-10, 16-26. Washington, DC: United States Conference of Catholic Bishops, 1988.

to say, a dialogue between the first and second part of its Bible" (Pope John Paul II, Mainz, November 17, 1980).

7. Another misunderstanding rejected by the Second Vatican Council was the notion of collective guilt, which charged the Jewish people *as a whole* with responsibility for Jesus' death (cf. nos. 21-25 below, on Holy Week). From the theory of collective guilt, it followed for some that Jewish suffering over the ages reflected divine retribution on the Jews for an alleged "deicide." While both rabbinic Judaism and early Christianity saw in the destruction of the Jerusalem Temple in A.D. 70 a sense of divine punishment (see Lk 19:42-44), the theory of collective guilt went well beyond Jesus' poignant expression of his love as a Jew for Jerusalem and the destruction it would face at the hands of Imperial Rome. Collective guilt implied that because "the Jews" had rejected Jesus, God had rejected them. With direct reference to Luke 19:44, the Second Vatican Council reminded Catholics that "nevertheless, now as before, God holds the Jews most dear for the sake of their fathers; he does not repent of the gifts he makes or of the calls he issues," and established as an overriding hermeneutical principle for homilists dealing with such passages that "the Jews should not be represented as rejected by God or accursed, as if this followed from Holy Scripture" (*Nostra Aetate*, no. 4; cf. 1985 *Notes*, VI:33).

8. Reasons for increased sensitivity to the ways in which Jews and Judaism are presented in homilies are multiple. First, understanding of the biblical readings and of the structure of Catholic liturgy will be enhanced by an appreciation of their ancient sources and their continuing spiritual links with Judaism. The Christian proclamation of the saving deeds of the One God through Jesus was formed in the context of Second Temple Judaism and cannot be understood thoroughly without that context. It is a proclamation that, at its heart, stands in solidarity with the continuing Jewish witness in affirming the One God as Lord of history. Further, false or demeaning portraits of a repudiated Israel may undermine Christianity as well. How can one confidently affirm the truth of God's covenant with all humanity and creation in Christ (see Rom 8:21) without at the same time affirming God's faithfulness to the Covenant with Israel that also lies at the heart of the biblical testimony?

9. As Catholic homilists know, the liturgical year presents both opportunities and challenges. One can show the parallels between the Jewish and Catholic liturgical cycles. And one can, with clarity, confront misinterpretations of the meaning of the lectionary readings, which have been too familiar in the past. Specifically, homilists can guide people away from a triumphalism that would equate the pilgrim Church with the Reign of God, which is the Church's mission to herald and proclaim. Likewise, homilists can confront the unconscious transmission of anti-Judaism through clichés that derive from an unhistorical overgeneralization of the self-critical aspects of the story of Israel as told in the Scriptures (e.g., "hardheartedness" of the Jews, 'blindness," "legalism," "materialism," "rejection of Jesus," etc.). From Advent through Passover/Easter, to Yom Kippur and Rosh Hashana, the Catholic and Jewish liturgical cycles spiral around one another in a stately progression of challenges to God's people to repent, to remain faithful to God's call, and to prepare the world for the coming of God's Reign. While each is distinct and unique, they are related to one another. Christianity is engrafted on and continues to draw sustenance from the common root, biblical Israel (Rom 11:13-24).

10. In this respect, the 1985 *Notes*, stressing "the unity of the divine plan" (no. 11), caution against a simplistic framing of the relationship of Christianity and Judaism as "two parallel ways of salvation" (no. 7). The Church proclaims the universal salvific significance of the Christ-event and looks forward to the day when "there shall be one flock and one shepherd" (Jn 10:16; cf. Is 66:2; Zep 3:9; Jet 23:3; Ez 11:17; see also no. 31e below). So intimate is this relationship that the Church "encounters the mystery of Israel" when "pondering her own mystery" (1974 *Guidelines*, no. 5).

LENT: CONTROVERSIES AND CONFLICTS

16. The Lenten lectionary presents just as many challenges. Prophetic texts such as Joel (Ash Wednesday), Jeremiah's "new covenant" (cycle B, Fifth Sunday), and Isaiah (cycle C, Fifth Sunday) call the assembly to proclaim Jesus as the Christ while avoiding negativism toward Judaism.

17. In addition, many of the New Testament texts, such as Matthew's references to "hypocrites in the synagogue" (Ash Wednesday), John's depiction of Jesus in the Temple (cycle B, Third Sunday), and Jesus' conflicts

with the Pharisees (e.g., Lk, cycle C, Fourth Sunday) can give the impression that the Judaism of Jesus' day was devoid of spiritual depth and essentially at odds with Jesus' teaching. References to earlier divine punishments of the Jews (e.g., 1 Cor, cycle C, Third Sunday) can further intensify a false image of Jews and Judaism as a people rejected by God.

18. In fact, however, as the 1985 *Notes* are at pains to clarify (sec. III and IV), Jesus was observant of the Torah (e.g., in the details of his circumcision and purification given in Lk 2:21-24), he extolled respect for it (see Mt 5:17-20), and he invited obedience to it (see Mt 8:4). Jesus taught in the synagogues (see Mt 4:23 and 9:35; Lk 4:15-18; Jn 18:20) and in the Temple, which he frequented, as did the disciples even after the Resurrection (see Acts 2:46; 3:1ff.). While Jesus showed uniqueness and authority in his interpretation of God's word in the Torah—in a manner that scandalized some Jews and impressed others—he did not oppose it, nor did he wish to abrogate it.

19. Jesus was perhaps closer to the Pharisees in his religious vision than to any other group of his time. The 1985 *Notes* suggest that this affinity with Pharisaism may be a reason for many of his apparent controversies with them (see no. 27). Jesus shared with the Pharisees a number of distinctive doctrines: the resurrection of the body; forms of piety such as almsgiving, daily prayer, and fasting; the liturgical practice of addressing God as Father; and the priority of the love commandment (see no. 25). Many scholars are of the view that Jesus was not so much arguing against "the Pharisees" as a group, as he was condemning excesses of some Pharisees, excesses of a sort that can be found among some Christians as well. In some cases, Jesus appears to have been participating in internal Pharisaic debates on various points of interpretation of God's law. In the case of divorce (see Mk 10:2-12), an issue that was debated hotly between the Pharisaic schools of Hillel and Shammai, Jesus goes beyond even the more stringent position of the House of Shammai. In other cases, such as the rejection of a literal interpretation of the *lex talionis* ("An eye for an eye. . . ."), Jesus' interpretation of biblical law is similar to that found in some of the prophets and ultimately adopted by rabbinic tradition as can be seen in the *Talmud*.

20. After the Church had distanced itself from Judaism (cf. no. 5 above), it tended to telescope the long historical process whereby the gospels were set

down some generations after Jesus' death. Thus, certain controversies that may actually have taken place between church leaders and rabbis toward the end of the first century were "read back" into the life of Jesus:

> Some [New Testament] references hostile or less than favorable to Jews have their historical context in conflicts between the nascent Church and the Jewish community. Certain controversies reflect Christian-Jewish relations long after the time of Jesus. To establish this is of capital importance if we wish to bring out the meaning of certain gospel texts for the Christians of today. All this should be taken into account when preparing catechesis and homilies for the weeks of Lent and Holy Week (1985 *Notes*, no. 29; see no. 26 below).

HOLY WEEK: THE PASSION NARRATIVES

21. Because of the tragic history of the "Christ-killer" charge as providing a rallying cry for anti-Semites over the centuries, a strong and careful homiletic stance is necessary to combat its lingering effects today. Homilists and catechists should seek to provide a proper context for the proclamation of the passion narratives. A particularly useful and detailed discussion of the theological and historical principles involved in presentations of the passions can be found in *Criteria for the Evaluation of Dramatizations of the Passion* issued by the Bishops' Committee for Ecumenical and Interreligious Affairs (March 1988).

22. The message of the liturgy in proclaiming the passion narratives in full is to enable the assembly to see vividly the love of Christ for each person, despite their sins, a love that even death could not vanquish. "Christ in his boundless love freely underwent his passion and death because of the sins of all so that all might attain salvation" (*Nostra Aetate*, no. 4). To the extent that Christians over the centuries made Jews the scapegoat for Christ's death, they drew themselves away from the paschal mystery. For it is only by dying to one's sins that we can hope to rise with Christ to new life. This is a central truth of the Catholic faith stated by the *Catechism* of the Council of Trent in the sixteenth century and reaffirmed by the 1985 *Notes* (no. 30).

23. It is necessary to remember that the passion narratives do not offer eyewitness accounts or a modern transcript of historical events. Rather, the

events have had their meaning focused, as it were, through the four theological "lenses" of the gospels. By comparing what is shared and what distinguishes the various gospel accounts from each other, the homilist can discern the core from the particular optics of each. One can then better see the significant theological differences between the passion narratives. These differences also are part of the inspired Word of God.

24. Certain historical essentials are shared by all four accounts: a growing hostility against Jesus on the part of some Jewish religious leaders (note that the Synoptic gospels do not mention the Pharisees as being involved in the events leading to Jesus' death, but only the "chief priests, scribes, and elders"); the Last Supper with the disciples; betrayal by Judas; arrest outside the city (an action conducted covertly by the Roman and Temple authorities because of Jesus' popularity among his fellow Jews); interrogation before a high priest (not necessarily a Sanhedrin trial); formal condemnation by Pontius Pilate (cf. the Apostles' and Nicene Creeds, which mention *only* Pilate, even though some Jews were involved); crucifixion by Roman soldiers; affixing the title "King of the Jews" on the cross; death; burial; and resurrection. Many other elements, such as the crowds shouting "His blood be on us and on our children" in Matthew, or the generic use of the term "the Jews" in John, are unique to a given author and must be understood within the context of that author's overall theological scheme. Often, these unique elements reflect the perceived needs and emphases of the author's particular community at the end of the first century, *after* the split between Jews and Christians was well underway. The bitterness toward synagogue Judaism seen in John's gospel (e.g., Jn 9:22; 16:2) most likely reflects the bitterness felt by John's own community after its "parting of the ways" with the Jewish community, and the martyrdom of St. Stephen illustrates that verbal disputes could, at times, lead to violence by Jews against fellow Jews who believed in Jesus.

25. Christian reflection on the passion should lead to a deep sense of the need for reconciliation with the Jewish community today. Pope John Paul II has said:

> Considering history in the light of the principles of faith in God,
> we must also reflect on the catastrophic event of the *Shoah*. . . .

Considering this mystery of the suffering of Israel's children, their witness of hope, of faith, and of humanity under dehumanizing outrages, the Church experiences ever more deeply her common bond with the Jewish people and with their treasure of spiritual riches in the past and in the present. (*Address to Jewish Leadership*, Miami, September 11, 1987)

THE EASTER SEASON

26. The readings of the Easter season, especially those from the book of Acts, which is used extensively throughout this liturgical period, require particular attention from the homilist in light of the enduring bond between Jews and Christians. Some of these readings from Acts (e.g., cycles A and B for the Third and Fourth Sundays of Easter) can leave an impression of collective Jewish responsibility for the crucifixion ("You put to death the author of life. . . ." Acts 3:15). In such cases, the homilist should put before the assembly the teachings of *Nostra Aetate* in this regard (see no. 22 above), as well as the fact noted in Acts 3:17 that what was done by some individual Jews was done "out of ignorance" so that no unwarranted conclusion about collective guilt is drawn by the hearers. The Acts may be dealing with a reflection of the Jewish-Christian relationship as it existed toward the end of the first century (when Acts was composed) rather than with the actual attitudes of the post-Easter Jerusalem Church. Homilists should desire to convey the spirit and enthusiasm of the early Church that marks these Easter season readings. But in doing so, statements about Jewish responsibility have to be kept in context. This is part of the reconciliation between Jews and Christians to which we are all called.

Criteria for the Evaluation of Dramatizations of the Passion

Bishops' Committee for Ecumenical and Interreligious Affairs
National Conference of Catholic Bishops
1988

PRELIMINARY CONSIDERATIONS

On June 24, 1985, the Vatican Commission for Religious Relations with the Jews issued *Notes on the Correct Way to Present the Jews and Judaism in Preaching and Catechesis of the Roman Catholic Church*. That document, like its predecessor, *Guidelines and Suggestions for Implementing the Conciliar Declaration "Nostra Aetate"* (no. 4) (December 1, 1974), drew its inspiration from the Second Vatican Council and was intended to be an offering on the part of the Holy See to Catholics on how the Conciliar mandate can properly be fulfilled "in our time."

The present document, in its turn, seeks to specify the catechetical principles established in the *Notes* with reference to depictions and presentations of the events surrounding the passion and death of Jesus, including but not limited to dramatic, staged presentations of Jesus' death most popularly known as "passion plays." The principles here invoked are applicable as the *Guidelines* suggest (ch. III) to "all levels of Christian instruction and education," whether written (textbooks, teachers' manuals, etc.) or oral (preaching, the mass media).

Specifically, the present document aims to provide practical applications regarding such presentations as they flow from the more general principles of the *Guidelines* and of sections III and IV of the *Notes* concerning the "Jewish Roots of Christianity" and the portrayal of "Jews in the New Testament." These principles (sec. A, below) lead to both negative and positive criteria (sec. B) for the evaluation of the many ways in which the Christian community throughout the world seeks, with commendable and pious intent, to remind itself of the universal significance and eternal spiritual challenge of the Savior's death and resurrection. A final section (C)

Bishops' Committee for Ecumenical and Interreligious Affairs, United States Conference of Catholic Bishops. *Criteria for the Evaluation of Dramatizations of the Passion*, 1-14. Washington, DC: United States Conference of Catholic Bishops, 1988.

acknowledges the many difficulties facing those attempting to dramatize the gospel narratives. It is hoped that this section will be helpful in providing perspectives on the many complex questions that can arise.

It has been noted by scholars that dramatizations of the passion were among the very last of the forms of "miracle" or "morality" plays to be developed in the Middle Ages. This hesitancy on the part of our ancestors in the faith can today only be regarded as most seemly, for the Church's primary reflection on the meaning of Jesus' death and resurrection takes place during Holy Week, as the high point of the liturgical cycle, and touches upon the most sacred and central mysteries of the faith.

It is all the more important, then, that extraliturgical depictions of the sacred mysteries conform to the highest possible standards of biblical interpretation and theological sensitivity. What is true of Catholic teaching in general is even more crucial with regard to depictions of Jesus' passion. In the words of Pope John Paul II as cited at the beginning of the *Notes*: "We should aim, in this field, that Catholic teaching at its different levels . . . presents Jews and Judaism, not only in an honest and objective manner, free from prejudices and without any offenses, but also with full awareness of the heritage common [to Jews and Christians]."

A. THE MYSTERY OF THE PASSION

1. The overall aim of any depiction of the passion should be the unambiguous presentation of the doctrinal understanding of the event in the light of faith, that is, of the Church's traditional interpretation of the meaning of Christ's death for all humanity. *Nostra Aetate* states this central gospel truth quite clearly: "Christ in his boundless love freely underwent his passion and death because of the sins of all, so that all might attain salvation" (cf. Notes IV, 30).

Therefore, any presentations that explicitly or implicitly seek to shift responsibility from human sin onto this or that historical group, such as the Jews, can only be said to obscure a core gospel truth. It has rightly been said that "correctly viewed, the disappearance of the charge of collective guilt of Jews pertains as much to the purity of the Catholic faith as it does to the defense of Judaism" (*Statement* of the National Conference of Catholic Bishops, November 20, 1975).

2. The question of *theological* responsibility for Jesus' death is a long settled one. From the theological perspective, the *Catechism* of the Council of Trent (cited in the *Notes* IV, 30) articulated without hesitancy what should be the major dramatic or moral focus of any dramatization of the event for Christians—a profound self-examination of our own guilt, through sin, for Jesus' death:

> In this guilt are involved all those who fall frequently into sin; for, as our sins consigned Christ the Lord to the death of the cross, most certainly those who wallow in sin and iniquity crucify to themselves again the Son of God. . . . This guilt seems more enormous in us than in the Jews since, if they had known it, they would never have crucified the Lord of glory; while we, on the contrary, professing to know him, yet denying him by our actions, seem in some sort to lay violent hands on him (*Catechism* of the Council of Trent).

3. The central creeds of the Church focus precisely on this theological message, without reference to the extremely complex historical question of reconstructing what various individuals might have done or not done. Only Pilate is mentioned, as the person with sole legal responsibility for the case: "He was also crucified for us, suffered under Pontius Pilate and was buried" (Nicene Creed). This fact gives a certain hermeneutic guidance for the use of various materials from the gospel passion narratives in a dramatic context (cf. sec. C, below).

4. In the development and evaluation of passion performances, then, the central criterion for judgment must be what the *Guidelines* called "an overriding preoccupation to bring out explicitly the *meaning* of the [gospel] text while taking scriptural studies into account" (II, emphasis added). Anything less than this "overriding preoccupation" to avoid caricaturing the Jewish people, which history has all too frequently shown us, will result almost inevitably in a violation of the basic hermeneutic principle of the Council in this regard: "the Jews should not be presented as rejected or accursed by God as if this followed from Sacred Scripture" (*Nostra Aetate*).

5. The 1985 *Notes* also provide a model for the positive understanding of the relationship between the Church and the Jewish people that should form a key element of the vision underlying presentations of the passion. As the *Notes* state: "The question is not merely to uproot from among the

faithful the remains of anti-Semitism still to be found here and there, but much rather to arouse in them, through educational work, an exact knowledge of the wholly unique 'bond' (*Nostra Aetate*, 4) which joins us as a Church to the Jews and to Judaism" (I, 8; cf. II, 10-11).

B. AVOIDING CARICATURES AND FALSE OPPOSITIONS

1. Any depiction of the death of Jesus will, to a greater or lesser extent, mix theological perspectives with historical reconstructions of the event based with greater or lesser fidelity on the four gospel accounts and what is known from extrabiblical records.

The nature of such mixtures leaves the widest possible latitude for artistic creativity and insight, but also for abuses and prejudices. What the *Notes* state in their conclusion regarding Christian-Jewish relations generally is equally, and perhaps especially, true of the history of the development of passion plays in their various forms: "There is evident, in particular, a painful ignorance of the history and traditions of Judaism, of which only negative aspects and often caricature seem to form part of the stock ideas of many Christians."

2. Judaism in the first century, especially, incorporated an extraordinarily rich and diverse set of groups and movements. Some sought a certain accommodation with Hellenic/Roman culture in the Diaspora and in the Land of Israel. Others vigorously opposed any cultural compromise, fearing ultimate religious assimilation. Some argued for armed rebellion against Rome (Zealots), others for peaceful but firm resistance to cultural oppression (some Pharisees) and a few, such as the Temple priesthood and its party (Sadducees) acted in the eyes of the people as collaborators with Rome.

Emotions and hopes (both practical and spiritual) ran high, and rhetoric often higher. Thus, along the lines of great issues of the day, and reacting to the pressure of Roman occupation, there moved a variety of groups, each with its own wide range of internal diversity: Sadducees, Zealots, apocalypticists, Pharisees (of varying dispositions, especially the two major schools of Hillel and Shammai), Herodians, Hellenists, scribes, sages, and miracle workers of all sorts. Scripture was understood variously: literally, mystically, allegorically, and through mediating principles of interpretation.

Jesus and his teachings can only be understood within this fluctuating mixture of Jewish trends and movements. In point of fact, various groups and leaders of Jesus' time (perhaps especially certain Pharisees) would have espoused many of Jesus' ideas, such as the nearness of the kingdom of God, resurrection of the body, opposition to the policies of the Temple, and so forth. The gospels reflect only some of this diversity. Succeeding generations of Christians, perhaps misconstruing the theological thrust of St. John's use of the term *Ioudaioi* ("the Jews" or "Judeans"), tended to flatten it into a monolithic, usually negative stereotype. Thus, caricature came to form the basis of the pejorative "stock ideas" rejected so forcefully by the *Notes*. Presentations of the passion, on the contrary, should strive to present the diversity of Jewish communities in Jesus' time, enabling viewers to understand that many of Jesus' major concerns (e.g., critique of Temple policies) would have been shared by other Jews of his time.

3. Many of these negative "stock ideas," unfortunately, can become vividly alive in passion dramatizations. It is all too easy in dramatic presentations to resort to artificial oppositions in order to heighten interest or provide sharp contrasts between the characters. Some of these erroneous oppositions, which are to be carefully avoided, are the following:

a.   Jesus must not be depicted as opposed to the Law (Torah). In fact, as the *Notes* describe in greater detail, "there is no doubt that he wished to submit himself to the law (Gal 4:4) . . . extolled respect for it" (Mt 5:17-20), and invited obedience to it" (Mt 8:4) (cf. *Notes* III, 21, 22). Jesus should be portrayed clearly as a pious, observant Jew of his time (*Notes* III, 20 and 28).

b.   The Old Testament and the Jewish tradition founded on it must not be set against the New Testament in such a way that the former seems to constitute a religion of only justice, fear, and legalism with no appeal to the love of God and neighbor (Dt 6:5; Lv 19:18; Mt 22:34-40; cf. *Guidelines* III).

c.   Jesus and the disciples must not be set dramatically in opposition to his people, the Jews. This is to misread, for example, the technical terminology employed by John's gospel (*Guidelines* II). It also ignores those parts of the gospel that show the Jewish populace well disposed toward Jesus. In his life and teaching, "Jesus was and always remained a Jew" (*Notes* III, 20), as, indeed, did the apostles (*Notes* III, 22).

d. Jews should not be portrayed as avaricious (e.g., in Temple money-changer scenes); blood thirsty (e.g., in certain depictions of Jesus' appearances before the Temple priesthood or before Pilate); or implacable enemies of Christ (e.g., by changing the small "crowd" at the governor's palace into a teeming mob). Such depictions, with their obvious "collective guilt" implications, eliminate those parts of the gospels that show that the secrecy surrounding Jesus' "trial" was motivated by the large following he had in Jerusalem and that the Jewish populace, far from wishing his death, would have opposed it had they known and, in fact, mourned his death by Roman execution (cf. Lk 23:27).

e. Any crowd or questioning scene, therefore, should reflect the fact that some in the crowd and among the Jewish leaders (e.g., Nicodemus, Joseph) supported Jesus and that the rest were manipulated by his opponents, as is made clear in the gospels (cf. *Nostra Aetate*, n. 4, "Jewish authorities"; *Notes* IV, 30).

f. Jesus and his teachings should not be portrayed as opposed to or by "the Pharisees" as a group (*Notes* III, 24). Jesus shared important Pharisaic doctrines (*Notes* III, 25) that set them apart from other Jewish groups of the time, such as the Sadducees. The Pharisees, in fact, are not mentioned in accounts of the passion except once in Luke, where Pharisees attempt to warn him of a plot against him by the followers of Herod (Lk 13:31). So, too, did a respected Pharisee, Gamaliel, speak out in a later time before the Sanhedrin to save the lives of the apostles (Acts 5). The Pharisees, therefore, should not be depicted as party to the proceedings against Jesus (*Notes* III, 24-27).

g. In sum, Judaism and Jewish society in the time of Christ and the apostles were complex realities, embracing many different trends, many spiritual, religious, social, and cultural values (*Guidelines* III). Presentations of the passion should strive to reflect this spiritual vitality, avoiding any implication that Jesus' death was a result of religious antagonism between a stereotyped "Judaism" and Christian doctrine. Many of the controversies (or "antitheses") between Jesus and his fellow Jews, as recorded in the gospels, we know today in fact reflect conflicts that took place long after the time of Christ between the early Christian communities and various Jewish communities (*Notes* IV, 29 A). To generalize from such specific and often later conflicts to an either/or opposition between Jesus and Judaism is to anachronize and, more basically, to vitiate the spirit and intent of the gospel texts (*Notes* III, 28; IV, 29 F).

h. In the light of the above criteria, it will also be useful to undertake a careful examination of the staging and costuming aspects of particular productions where this may apply. To give just one example, it is possible to project subtly yet powerfully any or all of the above "oppositions" by costuming: arraying Jesus' enemies in dark, sinister costuming and makeup, with Jesus and his friends in lighter tones. This can be effective on the stage. But it can also be disastrous if the effect is to isolate Jesus and the apostles from "the Jews," as if all were not part of the same people. It is important to portray Jesus and his followers clearly as Jews among Jews, both in dress and in actions such as prayer.

i. Similarly, the use of religious symbols requires careful evaluation. Displays of the menorah, tablets of the law, and other Jewish symbols should appear throughout the play and be connected with Jesus and his friends no less than with the Temple or with those opposed to Jesus. The presence of Roman soldiers should likewise be shown on the stage throughout the play, to represent the oppressive and pervasive nature of the Roman occupation.

C. DIFFICULTIES AND SENSITIVITIES IN HISTORICAL RECONSTRUCTION BASED ON THE FOUR GOSPEL ACCOUNTS

The mixture of theological, historical, and artistic aspects mentioned above (B 1) gives rise to many difficulties in constructing an adequate presentation of the passion narratives (Mt 26-28; Mk 14-15; Lk 22-23; Jn 18-19). Below are some examples of the difficult choices facing those who would seek to do so with faithfulness to the gospels. In each, an attempt will be made to apply to the question principles adduced in sections A and B, above, in the hope that such discussion will be of help to those charged with evaluations of the wide range of possible depictions existing today.

1. The Question of Selectivity

a. Those constructing a single narrative from the versions of the events in the four gospels are immediately aware that the texts differ in many details. To take just two examples, the famous phrase, "His Blood be upon us and on our children," exists only in the Matthean text (Mt 27:24-25), while the question of whether or not there was a full Sanhedrin trial is given widely differing interpretations in each of the gospel narratives. John, for example, has no Sanhedrin trial scene as such, but only a questioning before the two chief priests at dawn (18:19). Also in John, it is a Roman cohort, merely accompanied by Temple guards, that arrests Jesus (Jn 18:3, 12). How is one to choose between the differing versions?

b. First, it must be understood that the gospel authors did not intend to write "history" in our modern sense, but rather "sacred history" (i.e., offering "the honest truth about Jesus") (*Notes* IV, 29 A) in light of revelation. To attempt to utilize the four passion narratives literally by picking one passage from one gospel and the next from another gospel, and so forth, is to risk violating the integrity of the texts themselves, just as, for example, it violates the sense of Genesis 1 to reduce the magnificence of its vision of the Creation to a scientific theorem.

c. A clear and precise hermeneutic and a guiding artistic vision sensitive to historical fact and to the best biblical scholarship are obviously necessary. Just as obviously, it is not sufficient for the producers of passion dramatizations to respond to responsible criticism simply by appealing to the notion that "it's in the Bible." One must account for one's selections.

In the above instances, for example, one could take from John's gospel the phrase "the Jews" and mix it with Matthew 27:24-25, clearly implying a "blood guilt" on all Jews of all times in violation of *Nostra Aetate*'s dictum that "what happened in his passion cannot be blamed on all the Jews then living without distinction nor upon the Jews of today." Hence, if the Matthean phrase is to be used (not here recommended), great care would have to be taken throughout the presentation to ensure that such an interpretation does not prevail. Likewise, the historical and biblical questions surrounding the notion that there was a formal Sanhedrin trial argue for extreme caution and, perhaps, even abandoning the device. As a dramatic tool, it can too often lead to misunderstanding.

d. The greatest caution is advised in all cases where "it is a question of passages that seem to show the Jewish people as such in an unfavorable light" (*Guidelines* II). A general principle might, therefore, be suggested that if one cannot show beyond reasonable doubt that the particular gospel element selected or paraphrased will not be offensive or have the potential for negative influence on the audience for whom the presentation is intended, that element cannot, in good conscience, be used. This, admittedly, will be a difficult principle to apply. Yet, given what has been said above, it would seem to be a necessary one.

2. Historical Knowledge and Biblical Scholarship

a. Often, what we have come to know from biblical scholarship or historical studies will place in doubt a more literalist reading of the biblical text. Here again, the hermeneutical principles of *Nostra Aetate*, the *Guidelines*, and the *Notes* should be of "overriding" concern. One such question suggests itself by way of example. This is the portrait of Pontius Pilate (cf. sec. A 3, above). It raises a very real problem of methodology in historical reconstruction of the events of Jesus' last days.

b. *The Role of Pilate.* Certain of the gospels, especially the two latest ones, Matthew and John, seem on the surface to portray Pilate as a vacillating administrator who himself found "no fault" with Jesus and sought, though in a weak way, to free him. Other data from the gospels and secular sources contemporary with the events portray Pilate as a ruthless tyrant. We know from these latter sources that Pilate ordered crucified hundreds of Jews without proper trial under Roman law, and that in the year 36 Pilate was recalled to Rome to give an account. Luke, similarly, mentions "the Galileans whose blood Pilate mingled with their sacrifices" in the Temple (Lk 13:1-4), thus corroborating the contemporary secular accounts of the unusual cruelty of Pilate's administration. John, as mentioned above, is at pains to show that Jesus' arrest and trial were essentially at Roman hands. Finally, the gospels agree that Jesus' "crime," in Roman eyes, was that of political sedition—crucifixion being the Roman form of punishment for such charges. The threat to Roman rule is implicit in the charge: "King of the Jews," nailed to the cross at Pilate's order (Mt 27:37; Mk 15:26; Lk 23:38; Jn 19:19). Matthew 27:38 and Mark 15:27 identify the "criminals" crucified with Jesus on that day as "insurgents."

There is, then, room for more than one dramatic style of portraying the character of Pilate while still being faithful to the biblical record. Again, it is suggested here that the hermeneutical insight of *Nostra Aetate* and the use of the best available biblical scholarship cannot be ignored in the creative process and provide the most prudent and secure criterion for contemporary dramatic reconstructions.

CONCLUSION

The *Notes* emphasize that because the Church and the Jewish people are "linked together at the very level of their identity," an accurate, sensitive, and positive appreciation of Jews and Judaism "should not occupy an occasional or marginal place in Christian teaching," but be considered "essential" to Christian proclamation (I, 2; cf. I, 8).

This principle is nowhere more true than in depictions of the central events of the Paschal mystery. It is a principle that gives renewed urgency to the evaluation of all contemporary dramatizations of the passion and a renewed norm for undertaking that delicate and vital task.

APPENDIX

CATECHISM OF THE CATHOLIC CHURCH

Article 4: "Jesus Christ Suffered Under Pontius Pilate, Was Crucified, Died, and Was Buried"

PARAGRAPH 2. JESUS DIED CRUCIFIED

I. The Trial of Jesus

Divisions among the Jewish authorities concerning Jesus

595. Among the religious authorities of Jerusalem, not only were the Pharisee Nicodemus and the prominent Joseph of Arimathea both secret disciples of Jesus, but there was also long-standing dissension about him, so much so that St. John says of these authorities on the very eve of Christ's Passion, "many . . . believed in him," though very imperfectly.[378] This is not surprising, if one recalls that on the day after Pentecost "a great many of the priests were obedient to the faith" and "some believers . . . belonged to the party of the Pharisees," to the point that St. James could tell St. Paul, "How many thousands there are among the Jews of those who have believed; and they are all zealous for the Law."[379]

596. The religious authorities in Jerusalem were not unanimous about what stance to take toward Jesus.[380] The Pharisees threatened to excommunicate his followers.[381] To those who feared that "everyone will believe in him, and the Romans will come and destroy both our holy place and our nation," the high priest Caiaphas replied by prophesying: "It is expedient for you that one man should die for the people, and that the whole nation should not perish."[382] The Sanhedrin, having declared Jesus deserving of death as a blasphemer but having lost the right to put anyone to death, hands him over to the Romans, accusing him of political revolt, a charge that puts him in the same category as Barabbas who had been accused of sedition.[383] The high priests also threatened Pilate politically so that he would condemn Jesus to death.[384]

Catechism of the Catholic Church, 2d ed., nos. 595-598. Washington, DC: United States Conference of Catholic Bishops–Libreria Editrice Vaticana, 2000.

Jews are not collectively responsible for Jesus' death

597. The historical complexity of Jesus' trial is apparent in the Gospel accounts. The personal sin of the participants (Judas, the Sanhedrin, Pilate) is known to God alone. Hence we cannot lay responsibility for the trial on the Jews in Jerusalem as a whole, despite the outcry of a manipulated crowd and the global reproaches contained in the apostles' calls to conversion after Pentecost.[385] Jesus himself, in forgiving them on the cross, and Peter in following suit, both accept "the ignorance" of the Jews of Jerusalem and even of their leaders.[386] Still less can we extend responsibility to other Jews of different times and places, based merely on the crowd's cry: "His blood be on us and on our children!" a formula for ratifying a judicial sentence.[387] As the Church declared at the Second Vatican Council:

> . . . [N]either all Jews indiscriminately at that time, nor Jews today, can be charged with the crimes committed during his Passion. . . . [T]he Jews should not be spoken of as rejected or accursed as if this followed from holy Scripture.[388]

All sinners were the authors of Christ's Passion

598. In her Magisterial teaching of the faith and in the witness of her saints, the Church has never forgotten that "sinners were the authors and the ministers of all the sufferings that the divine Redeemer endured."[389] Taking into account the fact that our sins affect Christ himself,[390] the Church does not hesitate to impute to Christians the gravest responsibility for the torments inflicted upon Jesus, a responsibility with which they have all too often burdened the Jews alone:

> We must regard as guilty all those who continue to relapse into their sins. Since our sins made the Lord Christ suffer the torment of the cross, those who plunge themselves into disorders and crimes crucify the Son of God anew in their hearts (for he is in them) and hold him up to contempt. And it can be seen that our crime in this case is greater in us than in the Jews. As for them, according to the witness of the Apostle, "None of the rulers of this age understood this; for if they had, they would not have crucified

the Lord of glory." We, however, profess to know him. And when we deny him by our deeds, we in some way seem to lay violent hands on him.[391]

Nor did demons crucify him; it is you who have crucified him and crucify him still, when you delight in your vices and sins.[392]

Notes

378. Jn 12:42; cf. 7:50; 9:16-17; 10:19-21; 19:38-39.

379. Acts 6:7; 15:5; 21:20.

380. Cf. Jn 9:16; Jn 10:19.

381. Cf. Jn 9:22.

382. Jn 11:48-50.

383. Cf. Mt 26:66; Jn 18:31; Lk 23:2, 19.

384. Cf. Jn 19:12, 15, 21.

385. Cf. Mk 15:11; Acts 2:23, 36; 3:13-14; 4:10; 5:30; 7:52; 10:39; 13:27-28; 1 Thess 2:14-15.

386. Cf. Lk 23:34; Acts 3:17.

387. Mt 27:25; cf. Acts 5:28; 18:6.

388. NA 4.

389. *Roman Catechism* I, 5, 11; cf. Heb 12:3.

390. Cf. Mt 25:45; Acts 9:4-5.

391. *Roman Catechism* I, 5, 11; cf. Heb 6:6; 1 Cor 2:8.

392. St. Francis of Assisi, *Admonitio* 5, 3.

Papal Meditation on the First Station of the Cross

Rome, Good Friday, April 10, 1998

First Station

JESUS IS CONDEMNED TO DEATH

Pilate said to them, Then what should I do with Jesus who is called the Messiah? All of them said, Let him be crucified! Then he asked, Why, what evil has he done? they shouted all the more, Let him be crucified! So he released Barabbas for them; and after flogging Jesus, he handed him over to be crucified (Matt. 27:22-23, 26).

MEDITATION

Crucify him! The cry, reinforced by the blind passion of the crowd

—Strange liturgy of death—

it echoes throughout history.

It echoes throughout this century which is coming to a close, ashes of Auschwitz and ice of the Gulag, bloodied waters of the rice fields of Asia, of the lakes of Africa—paradises massacred.

So many children denied, prostituted, mutilated. Oh no, not the Jewish people, crucified by us for so long, not the crowd that will always prefer Barabbas, who he repays evil with evil, not them, but all of us, each one of us, because we are all murderers of love.

See how the Living One, in whom was not sown any seed of death, is condemned to death. The whip lacerates the body in which breathes the Spirit. They lead him out to be crucified.

"Prima Stazione, Gesù è condannato a morte," [First Station, Jesus is condemned to death] See http://www.vatican.va/holy_father/john_paul_ii/speeches/1998/april/documents/hf_jp-ii_hom_10041998_via-crucis_it.html?GRAB_ID=25\&EXTRA_ARG=\&HOST_ID=42\&PAGE_ID=6921216 (accessed January 31, 2004). [Translated from the Italian.]

GOSPEL NARRATIVES OF THE PASSION

The Passion of Our Lord Jesus Christ According to Matthew

Matthew 26:14–27:66

One of the Twelve, who was called Judas Iscariot, went to the chief priests and said, "What are you willing to give me if I hand him over to you?" They paid him thirty pieces of silver, and from that time on he looked for an opportunity to hand him over.

On the first day of the Feast of Unleavened Bread, the disciples approached Jesus and said, "Where do you want us to prepare for you to eat the Passover?" He said, "Go into the city to a certain man and tell him, 'The teacher says, "My appointed time draws near; in your house I shall celebrate the Passover with my disciples."'" The disciples then did as Jesus had ordered, and prepared the Passover.

When it was evening, he reclined at table with the Twelve. And while they were eating, he said, "Amen, I say to you, one of you will betray me." Deeply distressed at this, they began to say to him one after another, "Surely it is not I, Lord?" He said in reply, "He who has dipped his hand into the dish with me is the one who will betray me. The Son of Man indeed goes, as it is written of him, but woe to that man by whom the Son of Man is betrayed. It would be better for that man if he had never been born." Then Judas, his betrayer, said in reply, "Surely it is not I, Rabbi?" He answered, "You have said so."

While they were eating, Jesus took bread, said the blessing, broke it, and giving it to his disciples said, "Take and eat; this is my body." Then he took a cup, gave thanks, and gave it to them, saying, "Drink from it, all of you, for this is my blood of the covenant, which will be shed on behalf of many for the forgiveness of sins.

Lectionary for Mass, Second Typical Edition, volume I. Collegeville: The Liturgical Press, 1998.

I tell you, from now on I shall not drink this fruit of the vine until the day when I drink it with you new in the kingdom of my Father." Then, after singing a hymn, they went out to the Mount of Olives.

Then Jesus said to them, "This night all of you will have your faith in me shaken, for it is written:

> I will strike the shepherd,
>   and the sheep of the flock will be dispersed;

but after I have been raised up, I shall go before you to Galilee." Peter said to him in reply, "Though all may have their faith in you shaken, mine will never be." Jesus said to him, "Amen, I say to you, this very night before the cock crows, you will deny me three times." Peter said to him, "Even though I should have to die with you, I will not deny you." And all the disciples spoke likewise.

Then Jesus came with them to a place called Gethsemane, and he said to his disciples, "Sit here while I go over here and pray." He took along Peter and the two sons of Zebedee, and began to feel sorrow and distress. Then he said to them, "My soul is sorrowful even to death. Remain here and keep watch with me." He advanced a little and fell prostrate in prayer, saying, "My Father, if it is possible, let this cup pass from me; yet, not as I will, but as you will." When he returned to his disciples he found them asleep. He said to Peter, "So you could not keep watch with me for one hour? Watch and pray that you may not undergo the test. The spirit is willing, but the flesh is weak." Withdrawing a second time, he prayed again, "My Father, if it is not possible that this cup pass without my drinking it, your will be done!" Then he returned once more and found them asleep, for they could not keep their eyes open. He left them and withdrew again and prayed a third time, saying the same thing again. Then he returned to his disciples and said to them, "Are you still sleeping and taking your rest? Behold, the hour is at hand when the Son of Man is to be handed over to sinners. Get up, let us go. Look, my betrayer is at hand."

While he was still speaking, Judas, one of the Twelve, arrived, accompanied by a large crowd, with swords and clubs, who had come from the chief priests and the elders of the people. His betrayer had arranged a sign with them, saying, "The man I shall kiss is the one; arrest him." Immediately he went over to Jesus and said, "Hail, Rabbi!" and he kissed him. Jesus answered him, "Friend, do what you have come for." Then stepping forward they laid hands on Jesus and arrested him. And behold, one of those who accompanied Jesus put his hand to his sword, drew it, and struck the high priest's servant, cutting off his ear. Then Jesus said to him, "Put your sword back into its sheath, for all who take the sword will perish by the sword. Do you think that I cannot call upon my Father and he will not provide me at this moment with more than twelve legions of angels? But then how would the Scriptures be fulfilled which say that it must come to pass in this way?" At that hour Jesus said to the crowds, "Have you come out as against a robber, with swords and clubs to seize me? Day after day I sat teaching in the temple area, yet you did not arrest me. But all this has come to pass that the writings of the prophets may be fulfilled." Then all the disciples left him and fled.

Those who had arrested Jesus led him away to Caiaphas the high priest, where the scribes and the elders were assembled. Peter was following him at a distance as far as the high priest's courtyard, and going inside he sat down with the servants to see the outcome. The chief priests and the entire Sanhedrin kept trying to obtain false testimony against Jesus in order to put him to death, but they found none, though many false witnesses came forward. Finally two came forward who stated, "This man said, 'I can destroy the temple of God and within three days rebuild it.'" The high priest rose and addressed him, "Have you no answer? What are these men testifying against you?" But Jesus was silent. Then the high priest said to him, "I order you to tell us under oath before the living God whether you are the Christ, the Son of God." Jesus said to him in reply, "You have said so. But I tell you:

> From now on you will see 'the Son of Man
> seated at the right hand of the Power'
> and 'coming on the clouds of heaven.'"

Then the high priest tore his robes and said, "He has blasphemed! What further need have we of witnesses? You have now heard the blasphemy; what is your opinion?" They said in reply, "He deserves to die!" Then they spat in his face and struck him, while some slapped him, saying, "Prophesy for us, Christ: who is it that struck you?"

Now Peter was sitting outside in the courtyard. One of the maids came over to him and said, "You too were with Jesus the Galilean." But he denied it in front of everyone, saying, "I do not know what you are talking about!" As he went out to the gate, another girl saw him and said to those who were there, "This man was with Jesus the Nazorean." Again he denied it with an oath, "I do not know the man!" A little later the bystanders came over and said to Peter, "Surely you too are one of them; even your speech gives you away." At that he began to curse and to swear, "I do not know the man." And immediately a cock crowed. Then Peter remembered the word that Jesus had spoken: "Before the cock crows you will deny me three times."

He went out and began to weep bitterly.

When it was morning, all the chief priests and the elders of the people took counsel against Jesus to put him to death. They bound him, led him away, and handed him over to Pilate, the governor.

Then Judas, his betrayer, seeing that Jesus had been condemned, deeply regretted what he had done. He returned the thirty pieces of silver to the chief priests and elders, saying, "I have sinned in betraying innocent blood." They said, "What is that to us? Look to it yourself." Flinging the money into the temple, he departed and went off and hanged himself. The chief priests gathered up the money, but said, "It is not lawful to deposit this in the temple treasury, for it is the price of blood." After consultation, they used it to buy the potter's field as a burial place for foreigners. That is why that field even today is called the Field of Blood. Then was fulfilled what had been said through Jeremiah the prophet, *And they took the thirty pieces of silver, the value of a man with a price on his head, a price set by some of the Israelites, and they paid it out for the potter's field just as the Lord had commanded me.*

Now Jesus stood before the governor, and he questioned him, "Are you the king of the Jews?" Jesus said, "You say so." And when he was accused by the chief priests and elders, he made no answer. Then Pilate said to him, "Do you not hear how many things they are testifying against you?" But he did not answer him one word, so that the governor was greatly amazed.

Now on the occasion of the feast the governor was accustomed to release to the crowd one prisoner whom they wished. And at that time they had a notorious prisoner called Barabbas. So when they had assembled, Pilate said to them, "Which one do you want me to release to you, Barabbas, or Jesus called Christ?" For he knew that it was out of envy that they had handed him over. While he was still seated on the bench, his wife sent him a message, "Have nothing to do with that righteous man. I suffered much in a dream today because of him." The chief priests and the elders persuaded the crowds to ask for Barabbas but to destroy Jesus. The governor said to them in reply, "Which of the two do you want me to release to you?" They answered, "Barabbas!" Pilate said to them, "Then what shall I do with Jesus called Christ?" They all said, "Let him be crucified!" But he said, "Why? What evil has he done?" They only shouted the louder, "Let him be crucified!" When Pilate saw that he was not succeeding at all, but that a riot was breaking out instead, he took water and washed his hands in the sight of the crowd, saying, "I am innocent of this man's blood. Look to it yourselves." And the whole people said in reply, "His blood be upon us and upon our children." Then he released Barabbas to them, but after he had Jesus scourged, he handed him over to be crucified.

Then the soldiers of the governor took Jesus inside the praetorium and gathered the whole cohort around him. They stripped off his clothes and threw a scarlet military cloak about him. Weaving a crown out of thorns, they placed it on his head, and a reed in his right hand. And kneeling before him, they mocked him, saying, "Hail, King of the Jews!" They spat upon him and took the reed and kept striking him on the head. And when they had mocked him, they stripped him of the cloak, dressed him in his own clothes, and led him off to crucify him.

As they were going out, they met a Cyrenian named Simon; this man they pressed into service to carry his cross. And when they came to a place called Golgotha—which means Place of the Skull—they gave Jesus wine to drink mixed with gall. But when he had tasted it, he refused to drink. After they had crucified him, they divided his garments by casting lots; then they sat down and kept watch over him there. And they placed over his head the written charge against him: This is Jesus, the King of the Jews. Two revolutionaries were crucified with him, one on his right and the other on his left. Those passing by reviled him, shaking their heads and saying, "You who would destroy the temple and rebuild it in three days, save yourself, if you are the Son of God, and come down from the cross!" Likewise the chief priests with the scribes and elders mocked him and said, "He saved others; he cannot save himself. So he is the king of Israel! Let him come down from the cross now, and we will believe in him. He trusted in God; let him deliver him now if he wants him. For he said, 'I am the Son of God.'" The revolutionaries who were crucified with him also kept abusing him in the same way.

From noon onward, darkness came over the whole land until three in the afternoon. And about three o'clock Jesus cried out in a loud voice, *"Eli, Eli, lema sabachthani?"* which means, "My God, my God, why have you forsaken me?" Some of the bystanders who heard it said, "This one is calling for Elijah." Immediately one of them ran to get a sponge; he soaked it in wine, and putting it on a reed, gave it to him to drink. But the rest said, "Wait, let us see if Elijah comes to save him." But Jesus cried out again in a loud voice, and gave up his spirit.

And behold, the veil of the sanctuary was torn in two from top to bottom. The earth quaked, rocks were split, tombs were opened, and the bodies of many saints who had fallen asleep were raised. And coming forth from their tombs after his resurrection, they entered the holy city and appeared to many. The centurion and the men with him who were keeping watch over Jesus feared greatly when they saw the earthquake and all that was happening, and they said, "Truly, this was the Son of God!" There were many women there, looking on from a distance, who had followed Jesus from Galilee, ministering to him. Among them were Mary Magdalene and Mary the mother of James and Joseph, and the mother of the sons of Zebedee.

When it was evening, there came a rich man from Arimathea named Joseph, who was himself a disciple of Jesus. He went to Pilate and asked for the body of Jesus; then Pilate ordered it to be handed over. Taking the body, Joseph wrapped it in clean linen and laid it in his new tomb that he had hewn in the rock. Then he rolled a huge stone across the entrance to the tomb and departed. But Mary Magdalene and the other Mary remained sitting there, facing the tomb. The next day, the one following the day of preparation, the chief priests and the Pharisees gathered before Pilate and said, "Sir, we remember that this impostor while still alive said, 'After three days I will be raised up.' Give orders, then, that the grave be secured until the third day, lest his disciples come and steal him and say to the people, 'He has been raised from the dead.' This last imposture would be worse than the first." Pilate said to them, "The guard is yours; go, secure it as best you can." So they went and secured the tomb by fixing a seal to the stone and setting the guard.

The Passion of Our Lord Jesus Christ According to Mark

Mark 14:1–15:47

The Passover and the Feast of Unleavened Bread were to take place in two days' time. So the chief priests and the scribes were seeking a way to arrest him by treachery and put him to death. They said, "Not during the festival, for fear that there may be a riot among the people."

When he was in Bethany reclining at table in the house of Simon the leper, a woman came with an alabaster jar of perfumed oil, costly genuine spikenard. She broke the alabaster jar and poured it on his head. There were some who were indignant. "Why has there been this waste of perfumed oil? It could have been sold for more than three hundred days' wages and the money given to the poor." They were infuriated with her. Jesus said, "Let her alone. Why do you make trouble for her? She has done a good thing for me. The poor you will always have with you, and whenever you wish you can do good to them, but you will not always have me. She has done what she could. She has anticipated anointing my body for burial. Amen, I say to you, wherever the gospel is proclaimed to the whole world, what she has done will be told in memory of her."

Then Judas Iscariot, one of the Twelve, went off to the chief priests to hand him over to them. When they heard him they were pleased and promised to pay him money. Then he looked for an opportunity to hand him over.

On the first day of the Feast of Unleavened Bread, when they sacrificed the Passover lamb, his disciples said to him, "Where do you want us to go and prepare for you to eat the Passover?" He sent two of his disciples and said to them, "Go into the city and a man will meet you, carrying a jar of water. Follow him. Wherever he enters, say to the master of the house, 'The Teacher says, "Where is my guest room where I may eat the Passover with my disciples?"' Then he will show you a large upper room furnished and ready. Make the preparations for us there." The disciples then went off, entered the city, and found it just as he had told them; and they prepared the Passover.

When it was evening, he came with the Twelve. And as they reclined at table and were eating, Jesus said, "Amen, I say to you, one of you will betray me, one who is eating with me." They began to be distressed and to say to him, one by one, "Surely it is not I?" He said to them, "One of the Twelve, the one who dips with me into the dish. For the Son of Man indeed goes, as it is written of him, but woe to that man by whom the Son of Man is betrayed. It would be better for that man if he had never been born."

While they were eating, he took bread, said the blessing, broke it, and gave it to them, and said, "Take it; this is my body." Then he took a cup, gave thanks, and gave it to them, and they all drank from it. He said to them, "This is my blood of the covenant, which will be shed for many. Amen, I say to you, I shall not drink again the fruit of the vine until the day when I drink it new in the kingdom of God." Then, after singing a hymn, they went out to the Mount of Olives.

Then Jesus said to them, "All of you will have your faith shaken, for it is written:

> I will strike the shepherd,
>   and the sheep will be dispersed.

But after I have been raised up, I shall go before you to Galilee." Peter said to him, "Even though all should have their faith shaken, mine will not be." Then Jesus said to him, "Amen, I say to you, this very night before the cock crows twice you will deny me three times." But he vehemently replied, "Even though I should have to die with you, I will not deny you." And they all spoke similarly. Then they came to a place named Gethsemane, and he said to his disciples, "Sit here while I pray." He took with him Peter, James, and John, and began to be troubled and distressed. Then he said to them, "My soul is sorrowful even to death. Remain here and keep watch." He advanced a little and fell to the ground and prayed that if it were possible the hour might pass by him; he said, "Abba, Father, all things are possible to you. Take this cup away from me, but not what I will but what you will."

When he returned he found them asleep. He said to Peter, "Simon, are you asleep? Could you not keep watch for one hour? Watch and pray that you may not undergo the test. The spirit is willing but the flesh is weak."

Withdrawing again, he prayed, saying the same thing. Then he returned once more and found them asleep, for they could not keep their eyes open and did not know what to answer him. He returned a third time and said to them, "Are you still sleeping and taking your rest? It is enough. The hour has come. Behold, the Son of Man is to be handed over to sinners. Get up, let us go. See, my betrayer is at hand."

Then, while he was still speaking, Judas, one of the Twelve, arrived, accompanied by a crowd with swords and clubs who had come from the chief priests, the scribes, and the elders. His betrayer had arranged a signal with them, saying, "The man I shall kiss is the one; arrest him and lead him away securely." He came and immediately went over to him and said, "Rabbi." And he kissed him. At this they laid hands on him and arrested him. One of the bystanders drew his sword, struck the high priest's servant, and cut off his ear.

Jesus said to them in reply, "Have you come out as against a robber, with swords and clubs, to seize me?

Day after day I was with you teaching in the temple area, yet you did not arrest me; but that the Scriptures may be fulfilled." And they all left him and fled. Now a young man followed him wearing nothing but a linen cloth about his body. They seized him, but he left the cloth behind and ran off naked.

They led Jesus away to the high priest, and all the chief priests and the elders and the scribes came together.

Peter followed him at a distance into the high priest's courtyard and was seated with the guards, warming himself at the fire. The chief priests and the entire Sanhedrin kept trying to obtain testimony against Jesus in order to put him to death, but they found none. Many gave false witness against him, but their testimony did not agree. Some took the stand and testified falsely against him, alleging, "We heard him say, 'I will destroy this temple made with hands and within three days I will build another not made with hands.'" Even so their testimony did not agree. The high priest rose before the assembly and questioned Jesus, saying, "Have you no answer? What are these men testifying against you?" But he was silent and answered nothing.

Again the high priest asked him and said to him, "Are you the Christ, the son of the Blessed One?" Then Jesus answered, "I am;

> and 'you will see the Son of Man
> seated at the right hand of the Power
> and coming with the clouds of heaven.'"

At that the high priest tore his garments and said, "What further need have we of witnesses? You have heard the blasphemy. What do you think?" They all condemned him as deserving to die. Some began to spit on him. They blindfolded him and struck him and said to him, "Prophesy!" And the guards greeted him with blows.

While Peter was below in the courtyard, one of the high priest's maids came along. Seeing Peter warming himself, she looked intently at him and said, "You too were with the Nazarene, Jesus." But he denied it saying, "I neither know nor understand what you are talking about." So he went out into the outer court. Then the cock crowed. The maid saw him and began again to say to the bystanders, "This man is one of them." Once again he denied it. A little later the bystanders said to Peter once more, "Surely you are one of them; for you too are a Galilean." He began to curse and to swear, "I do not know this man about whom you are talking." And immediately a cock crowed a second time. Then Peter remembered the word that Jesus had said to him, "Before the cock crows twice you will deny me three times." He broke down and wept.

As soon as morning came, the chief priests with the elders and the scribes, that is, the whole Sanhedrin held a council. They bound Jesus, led him away, and handed him over to Pilate. Pilate questioned him, "Are you the king of the Jews?" He said to him in reply, "You say so." The chief priests accused him of many things. Again Pilate questioned him, "Have you no answer? See how many things they accuse you of." Jesus gave him no further answer, so that Pilate was amazed.

Now on the occasion of the feast he used to release to them one prisoner whom they requested. A man called Barabbas was then in prison along with the rebels who had committed murder in a rebellion. The crowd came forward and began to ask him to do for them as he was accustomed. Pilate answered, "Do you want me to release to you the king of the Jews?" For he knew that it was out of envy that the chief priests had handed him over. But the chief priests stirred up the crowd to have him release Barabbas for them instead. Pilate again said to them in reply, "Then what do you want me to do with the man you call the king of the Jews?" They shouted again, "Crucify him." Pilate said to them, "Why? What evil has he done?" They only shouted the louder, "Crucify him." So Pilate, wishing to satisfy the crowd, released Barabbas to them and, after he had Jesus scourged, handed him over to be crucified.

The soldiers led him away inside the palace, that is, the praetorium, and assembled the whole cohort. They clothed him in purple and, weaving a crown of thorns, placed it on him. They began to salute him with, "Hail, King of the Jews!" and kept striking his head with a reed and spitting upon him. They knelt before him in homage. And when they had mocked him, they stripped him of the purple cloak, dressed him in his own clothes, and led him out to crucify him.

They pressed into service a passer-by, Simon, a Cyrenian, who was coming in from the country, the father of Alexander and Rufus, to carry his cross.

They brought him to the place of Golgotha (which is translated Place of the Skull). They gave him wine drugged with myrrh, but he did not take it. Then they crucified him and divided his garments by casting lots for them to see what each should take. It was nine o'clock in the morning when they crucified him. The inscription of the charge against him read, "The King of the Jews." With him they crucified two revolutionaries, one on his right and one on his left. Those passing by reviled him, shaking their heads and saying, "Aha! You who would destroy the temple and rebuild it in three days, save yourself by coming down from the cross." Likewise the chief priests, with the scribes, mocked him among themselves and said, "He saved others; he cannot save himself. Let the Christ, the King of Israel, come down now from the cross that we may see and believe." Those who were crucified with him also kept abusing him. At noon darkness came over the whole land until three in the afternoon. And at three o'clock Jesus cried out in a loud voice, *"Eloi, Eloi, lema sabachthani?"* which is translated, "My God, my God, why have you forsaken me?" Some of the bystanders who heard it said, "Look, he is calling Elijah." One of them ran, soaked a sponge with wine, put it on a reed and gave it to him to drink saying, "Wait, let us see if Elijah comes to take him down." Jesus gave a loud cry and breathed his last.

The veil of the sanctuary was torn in two from top to bottom. When the centurion who stood facing him saw how he breathed his last he said, "Truly this man was the Son of God!" There were also women looking on from a distance. Among them were Mary Magdalene, Mary the mother of the younger James and of Joses, and Salome. These women had followed him when he was in Galilee and ministered to him. There were also many other women who had come up with him to Jerusalem.

When it was already evening, since it was the day of preparation, the day before the sabbath, Joseph of Arimathea, a distinguished member of the council, who was himself awaiting the kingdom of God, came and courageously went to Pilate and asked for the body of Jesus. Pilate was amazed that he was already dead.

He summoned the centurion and asked him if Jesus had already died. And when he learned of it from the centurion, he gave the body to Joseph. Having bought a linen cloth, he took him down, wrapped him in the linen cloth, and laid him in a tomb that had been hewn out of the rock. Then he rolled a stone against the entrance to the tomb. Mary Magdalene and Mary the mother of Joses watched where he was laid.

The Passion of Our Lord Jesus Christ According to Luke

Luke 22:14–23:56

When the hour came, Jesus took his place at table with the apostles. He said to them, "I have eagerly desired to eat this Passover with you before I suffer, for, I tell you, I shall not eat it again until there is fulfillment in the kingdom of God." Then he took a cup, gave thanks, and said, "Take this and share it among yourselves; for I tell you that from this time on I shall not drink of the fruit of the vine until the kingdom of God comes." Then he took the bread, said the blessing, broke it, and gave it to them, saying, "This is my body, which will be given for you; do this in memory of me." And likewise the cup after they had eaten, saying, "This cup is the new covenant in my blood, which will be shed for you.

"And yet behold, the hand of the one who is to betray me is with me on the table; for the Son of Man indeed goes as it has been determined; but woe to that man by whom he is betrayed." And they began to debate among themselves who among them would do such a deed.

Then an argument broke out among them about which of them should be regarded as the greatest. He said to them, "The kings of the Gentiles lord it over them and those in authority over them are addressed as 'Benefactors'; but among you it shall not be so. Rather, let the greatest among you be as the youngest, and the leader as the servant. For who is greater: the one seated at table or the one who serves? Is it not the one seated at table? I am among you as the one who serves. It is you who have stood by me in my trials; and I confer a kingdom on you, just as my Father has conferred one on me, that you may eat and drink at my table in my kingdom; and you will sit on thrones judging the twelve tribes of Israel.

"Simon, Simon, behold Satan has demanded to sift all of you like wheat, but I have prayed that your own faith may not fail; and once you have turned back, you must strengthen your brothers." He said to him, "Lord, I am prepared to go to prison and to die with you." But he replied, "I tell you, Peter, before the cock crows this day, you will deny three times that you know me."

He said to them, "When I sent you forth without a money bag or a sack or sandals, were you in need of anything?" "No, nothing," they replied. He said to them, "But now one who has a money bag should take it, and likewise a sack, and one who does not have a sword should sell his cloak and buy one. For I tell you that this Scripture must be fulfilled in me, namely, *He was counted among the wicked*; and indeed what is written about me is coming to fulfillment." Then they said, "Lord, look, there are two swords here." But he replied, "It is enough!"

Then going out, he went, as was his custom, to the Mount of Olives, and the disciples followed him. When he arrived at the place he said to them, "Pray that you may not undergo the test." After withdrawing about a stone's throw from them and kneeling, he prayed, saying, "Father, if you are willing, take this cup away from me; still, not my will but yours be done." And to strengthen him an angel from heaven appeared to him. He was in such agony and he prayed so fervently that his sweat became like drops of blood falling on the ground. When he rose from prayer and returned to his disciples, he found them sleeping from grief. He said to them, "Why are you sleeping? Get up and pray that you may not undergo the test."

While he was still speaking, a crowd approached and in front was one of the Twelve, a man named Judas.

He went up to Jesus to kiss him. Jesus said to him, "Judas, are you betraying the Son of Man with a kiss?"

His disciples realized what was about to happen, and they asked, "Lord, shall we strike with a sword?"

And one of them struck the high priest's servant and cut off his right ear. But Jesus said in reply, "Stop, no more of this!" Then he touched the servant's ear and healed him. And Jesus said to the chief priests and temple guards and elders who had come for him, "Have you come out as against a robber, with swords and clubs? Day after day I was with you in the temple area, and you did not seize me; but this is your hour, the time for the power of darkness."

After arresting him they led him away and took him into the house of the high priest; Peter was following at a distance. They lit a fire in the middle of the courtyard and sat around it, and Peter sat down with them. When a maid saw him seated in the light, she looked intently at him and said, "This man too was with him." But he denied it saying, "Woman, I do not know him." A short while later someone else saw him and said, "You too are one of them"; but Peter answered, "My friend, I am not." About an hour later, still another insisted, "Assuredly, this man too was with him, for he also is a Galilean." But Peter said, "My friend, I do not know what you are talking about." Just as he was saying this, the cock crowed, and the Lord turned and looked at Peter; and Peter remembered the word of the Lord, how he had said to him, "Before the cock crows today, you will deny me three times." He went out and began to weep bitterly.

The men who held Jesus in custody were ridiculing and beating him. They blindfolded him and questioned him, saying, "Prophesy! Who is it that struck you?" And they reviled him in saying many other things against him.

When day came the council of elders of the people met, both chief priests and scribes, and they brought him before their Sanhedrin. They said, "If you are the Christ, tell us," but he replied to them, "If I tell you, you will not believe, and if I question, you will not respond. But from this time on the Son of Man will be seated at the right hand of the power of God." They all asked, "Are you then the Son of God?" He replied to them, "You say that I am." Then they said, "What further need have we for testimony? We have heard it from his own mouth."

Then the whole assembly of them arose and brought him before Pilate. They brought charges against him, saying, "We found this man misleading our people; he opposes the payment of taxes to Caesar and maintains that he is the Christ, a king." Pilate asked him, "Are you the king of the Jews?" He said to him in reply, "You say so." Pilate then addressed the chief priests and the crowds, "I find this man not guilty." But they were adamant and said, "He is inciting the people with his teaching throughout all Judea, from Galilee where he began even to here."

On hearing this Pilate asked if the man was a Galilean; and upon learning that he was under Herod's jurisdiction, he sent him to Herod who was in Jerusalem at that time. Herod was very glad to see Jesus; he had been wanting to see him for a long time, for he had heard about him and had been hoping to see him perform some sign. He questioned him at length, but he gave him no answer. The chief priests and scribes, meanwhile, stood by accusing him harshly. Herod and his soldiers treated him contemptuously and mocked him, and after clothing him in resplendent garb, he sent him back to Pilate. Herod and Pilate became friends that very day, even though they had been enemies formerly. Pilate then summoned the chief priests, the rulers, and the people and said to them, "You brought this man to me and accused him of inciting the people to revolt. I have conducted my investigation in your presence and have not found this man guilty of the charges you have brought against him, nor did Herod, for he sent him back to us. So no capital crime has been committed by him. Therefore I shall have him flogged and then release him."

But all together they shouted out, "Away with this man! Release Barabbas to us." (Now Barabbas had been imprisoned for a rebellion that had taken place in the city and for murder.) Again Pilate addressed them, still wishing to release Jesus, but they continued their shouting, "Crucify him! Crucify him!" Pilate addressed them a third time, "What evil has this man done? I found him guilty of no capital crime. Therefore I shall have him flogged and then release him." With loud shouts, however, they persisted in calling for his crucifixion, and their voices prevailed. The verdict of Pilate was that their demand should be granted. So he released the man who had been imprisoned for rebellion and murder, for whom they asked, and he handed Jesus over to them to deal with as they wished.

As they led him away they took hold of a certain Simon, a Cyrenian, who was coming in from the country; and after laying the cross on him, they made him carry it behind Jesus. A large crowd of people followed Jesus, including many women who mourned and lamented him. Jesus turned to them and said, "Daughters of Jerusalem, do not weep for me; weep instead for yourselves and for your children for indeed, the days are coming when people will say, 'Blessed are the barren, the wombs that never bore and the breasts that never nursed.' At that time people will say to the mountains, 'Fall upon us!' and to the hills, 'Cover us!' for if these things are done when the wood is green what will happen when it is dry?" Now two others, both criminals, were led away with him to be executed.

When they came to the place called the Skull, they crucified him and the criminals there, one on his right, the other on his left. Then Jesus said, "Father, forgive them, they know not what they do." They divided his garments by casting lots. The people stood by and watched; the rulers, meanwhile, sneered at him and said, "He saved others, let him save himself if he is the chosen one, the Christ of God." Even the soldiers jeered at him.

As they approached to offer him wine they called out, "If you are King of the Jews, save yourself." Above him there was an inscription that read, "This is the King of the Jews."

Now one of the criminals hanging there reviled Jesus, saying, "Are you not the Christ? Save yourself and us." The other, however, rebuking him, said in reply, "Have you no fear of God, for you are subject to the same condemnation? And indeed, we have been condemned justly, for the sentence we received corresponds to our crimes, but this man has done nothing criminal." Then he said, "Jesus, remember me when you come into your kingdom." He replied to him, "Amen, I say to you, today you will be with me in Paradise."

It was now about noon and darkness came over the whole land until three in the afternoon because of an eclipse of the sun. Then the veil of the temple was torn down the middle. Jesus cried out in a loud voice, "Father, into your hands I commend my spirit"; and when he had said this he breathed his last. The centurion who witnessed what had happened glorified God and said, "This man was innocent beyond doubt."

When all the people who had gathered for this spectacle saw what had happened, they returned home beating their breasts; but all his acquaintances stood at a distance, including the women who had followed him from Galilee and saw these events.

Now there was a virtuous and righteous man named Joseph who, though he was a member of the council, had not consented to their plan of action. He came from the Jewish town of Arimathea and was awaiting the kingdom of God. He went to Pilate and asked for the body of Jesus. After he had taken the body down, he wrapped it in a linen cloth and laid him in a rock-hewn tomb in which no one had yet been buried. It was the day of preparation, and the sabbath was about to begin. The women who had come from Galilee with him followed behind, and when they had seen the tomb and the way in which his body was laid in it, they returned and prepared spices and perfumed oils. Then they rested on the sabbath according to the commandment.

The Passion of Our Lord Jesus Christ According to John

John 18:1–19:42

Jesus went out with his disciples across the Kidron valley to where there was a garden, into which he and his disciples entered. Judas his betrayer also knew the place, because Jesus had often met there with his disciples.

So Judas got a band of soldiers and guards from the chief priests and the Pharisees and went there with lanterns, torches, and weapons. Jesus, knowing everything that was going to happen to him, went out and said to them, "Whom are you looking for?" They answered him, "Jesus the Nazorean." He said to them, "I AM." Judas his betrayer was also with them. When he said to them, "I AM, " they turned away and fell to the ground. So he again asked them, "Whom are you looking for?" They said, "Jesus the Nazorean." Jesus answered, "I told you that I AM. So if you are looking for me, let these men go." This was to fulfill what he had said, "I have not lost any of those you gave me." Then Simon Peter, who had a sword, drew it, struck the high priest's slave, and cut off his right ear. The slave's name was Malchus. Jesus said to Peter, "Put your sword into its scabbard. Shall I not drink the cup that the Father gave me?"

So the band of soldiers, the tribune, and the Jewish guards seized Jesus, bound him, and brought him to Annas first. He was the father-in-law of Caiaphas, who was high priest that year. It was Caiaphas who had counseled the Jews that it was better that one man should die rather than the people.

Simon Peter and another disciple followed Jesus. Now the other disciple was known to the high priest, and he entered the courtyard of the high priest with Jesus. But Peter stood at the gate outside. So the other disciple, the acquaintance of the high priest, went out and spoke to the gatekeeper and brought Peter in. Then the maid who was the gatekeeper said to Peter, "You are not one of this man's disciples, are you?" He said, "I am not." Now the slaves and the guards were standing around a charcoal fire that they had made, because it was cold, and were warming themselves. Peter was also standing there keeping warm.

The high priest questioned Jesus about his disciples and about his doctrine. Jesus answered him, "I have spoken publicly to the world. I have always taught in a synagogue or in the temple area where all the Jews gather, and in secret I have said nothing. Why ask me? Ask those who heard me what I said to them. They know what I said." When he had said this, one of the temple guards standing there struck Jesus and said, "Is this the way you answer the high priest?" Jesus answered him, "If I have spoken wrongly, testify to the wrong; but if I have spoken rightly, why do you strike me?" Then Annas sent him bound to Caiaphas the high priest.

Now Simon Peter was standing there keeping warm. And they said to him, "You are not one of his disciples, are you?" He denied it and said, "I am not." One of the slaves of the high priest, a relative of the one whose ear Peter had cut off, said, "Didn't I see you in the garden with him?" Again Peter denied it. And immediately the cock crowed.

Then they brought Jesus from Caiaphas to the praetorium. It was morning. And they themselves did not enter the praetorium, in order not to be defiled so that they could eat the Passover. So Pilate came out to them and said, "What charge do you bring against this man?" They answered and said to him, "If he were not a criminal, we would not have handed him over to you." At this, Pilate said to them, "Take him yourselves, and judge him according to your law." The Jews answered him, "We do not have the right to execute anyone," in order that the word of Jesus might be fulfilled that he said indicating the kind of death he would die. So Pilate went back into the praetorium and summoned Jesus and said to him, "Are you the King of the Jews?" Jesus answered, "Do you say this on your own or have others told you about me?" Pilate answered, "I am not a Jew, am I? Your own nation and the chief priests handed you over to me. What have you done?" Jesus answered, "My kingdom does not belong to this world. If my kingdom did belong to this world, my attendants would be fighting to keep me from being handed over to the Jews. But as it is, my kingdom is not here." So Pilate said to him, "Then you are a king?" Jesus answered, "You say I am a king. For this I was born and for this I came into the world, to testify to the truth. Everyone who belongs to the truth listens to my voice." Pilate said to him, "What is truth?"

When he had said this, he again went out to the Jews and said to them, "I find no guilt in him. But you have a custom that I release one prisoner to you at Passover. Do you want me to release to you the King of the Jews?"

They cried out again, "Not this one but Barabbas!" Now Barabbas was a revolutionary.

Then Pilate took Jesus and had him scourged. And the soldiers wove a crown out of thorns and placed it on his head, and clothed him in a purple cloak, and they came to him and said, "Hail, King of the Jews!" And they struck him repeatedly. Once more Pilate went out and said to them, "Look, I am bringing him out to you, so that you may know that I find no guilt in him." So Jesus came out, wearing the crown of thorns and the purple cloak. And he said to them, "Behold, the man!" When the chief priests and the guards saw him they cried out, "Crucify him, crucify him!" Pilate said to them, "Take him yourselves and crucify him. I find no guilt in him."

The Jews answered, "We have a law, and according to that law he ought to die, because he made himself the Son of God." Now when Pilate heard this statement, he became even more afraid, and went back into the praetorium and said to Jesus, "Where are you from?" Jesus did not answer him. So Pilate said to him, "Do you not speak to me? Do you not know that I have power to release you and I have power to crucify you?" Jesus answered him, "You would have no power over me if it had not been given to you from above. For this reason the one who handed me over to you has the greater sin." Consequently, Pilate tried to release him; but the Jews cried out, "If you release him, you are not a Friend of Caesar. Everyone who makes himself a king opposes Caesar."

When Pilate heard these words he brought Jesus out and seated him on the judge's bench in the place called Stone Pavement, in Hebrew, Gabbatha. It was preparation day for Passover, and it was about noon. And he said to the Jews, "Behold, your king!" They cried out, "Take him away, take him away! Crucify him!" Pilate said to them, "Shall I crucify your king?" The chief priests answered, "We have no king but Caesar." Then he handed him over to them to be crucified.

So they took Jesus, and, carrying the cross himself, he went out to what is called the Place of the Skull, in Hebrew, Golgotha. There they crucified him, and with him two others, one on either side, with Jesus in the middle. Pilate also had an inscription written and put on the cross. It read, "Jesus the Nazorean, the King of the Jews." Now many of the Jews read this inscription, because the place where Jesus was crucified was near the city; and it was written in Hebrew, Latin, and Greek. So the chief priests of the Jews said to Pilate, "Do not write 'The King of the Jews,' but that he said, 'I am the King of the Jews.'" Pilate answered, "What I have written, I have written."

When the soldiers had crucified Jesus, they took his clothes and divided them into four shares, a share for each soldier. They also took his tunic, but the tunic was seamless, woven in one piece from the top down. So they said to one another, "Let's not tear it, but cast lots for it to see whose it will be," in order that the passage of Scripture might be fulfilled that says:

> They divided my garments among them,
> and for my vesture they cast lots.

This is what the soldiers did. Standing by the cross of Jesus were his mother and his mother's sister, Mary the wife of Clopas, and Mary of Magdala. When Jesus saw his mother and the disciple there whom he loved he said to his mother, "Woman, behold, your son." Then he said to the disciple, "Behold, your mother." And from that hour the disciple took her into his home.

After this, aware that everything was now finished, in order that the Scripture might be fulfilled, Jesus said, "I thirst." There was a vessel filled with common wine. So they put a sponge soaked in wine on a sprig of hyssop and put it up to his mouth. When Jesus had taken the wine, he said, "It is finished." And bowing his head, he handed over the spirit.

Now since it was preparation day, in order that the bodies might not remain on the cross on the sabbath, for the sabbath day of that week was a solemn one, the Jews asked Pilate that their legs be broken and that they be taken down. So the soldiers came and broke the legs of the first and then of the other one who was crucified with Jesus. But when they came to Jesus and saw that he was already dead, they did not break his legs, but one soldier thrust his lance into his side, and immediately blood and water flowed out. An eyewitness has testified, and his testimony is true; he knows that he is speaking the truth, so that you also may come to believe. For this happened so that the Scripture passage might be fulfilled:

> Not a bone of it will be broken.

And again another passage says:

They will look upon him whom they have pierced.

After this, Joseph of Arimathea, secretly a disciple of Jesus for fear of the Jews, asked Pilate if he could remove the body of Jesus. And Pilate permitted it. So he came and took his body. Nicodemus, the one who had first come to him at night, also came bringing a mixture of myrrh and aloes weighing about one hundred pounds. They took the body of Jesus and bound it with burial cloths along with the spices, according to the Jewish burial custom. Now in the place where he had been crucified there was a garden, and in the garden a new tomb, in which no one had yet been buried. So they laid Jesus there because of the Jewish preparation day; for the tomb was close by.

ADDITIONAL RESOURCES AVAILABLE ON JEWISH-CATHOLIC RELATIONS

Walking God's Paths
Christians and Jews in Candid Conversation
Six 15-minute discussion-starting segments are perfect for understanding how Christians and Jews can relate to one another in positive ways. This video is a great resource for adult education, ecumenical officers, and interfaith marriage counselors.
No. 5-596, 90 min. video

Catholic Teaching on the Shoah
Implementing the Holy See's "We Remember"
The bishops offer ways to frame Holocaust issues properly and sensitively for Catholic students using historical and theological contexts. Additional included resources provide aid in developing curricula and furthering dialogue.
No. 5-406, 32 pp.

Catholics Remember the Holocaust
Centering on the Vatican statement "We Remember: A Reflection on the *Shoah*," issued by the Commission for Religious Relations with the Jews, this publication includes the full text of the document, with introduction and commentaries. A bibliography is included.
No. 5-290, 84 pp.

Catholic Jewish Relations
Documents from the Holy See
This important collection includes the *Declarations on the Relationships of the Church to Non-Christian Religions (Nostra Aetate), Guidelines and suggestions for Implementing the Conciliar Declaration "Nostra Aetate," Notes on the Correct Way to Present Jews and Judaism in Preaching and Catechesis in the Roman Catholic Church,* and *We Remember: A Reflection on the Shoah.*
No. 062-X, 88 pp.

God's Mercy Endures Forever
Guidelines on the Presentation of Jews and Judaism in Catholic Preaching
No. 247-0, 24 pp.

On Jews and Judaism, 1979-1986
Compilation of reflections from Pope John Paul II.
No. 151-2, 97 pp.

To order these resources or to obtain a catalog of other USCCB titles, call toll-free 800-235-8722. In the Washington metropolitan area or from outside the United States, call 202-722-8716. Visit the bishops' Internet site at *www.usccb.org*. Para ordenar recursos en español, llame al 800-235-8722 y presione 4 para hablar con un representante del servicio al cliente en español.